A better way

By the same author
The Christian in Industrial Society (IVP)
The Christian Citizen (Hodder and Stoughton)

To Christopher

Inter-Varsity Press

A better way

The case for a Christian social order
Sir Frederick Catherwood

© INTER-VARSITY PRESS, LEICESTER, ENGLAND

Universities and Colleges Christian Fellowship
38 De Montfort Street, Leicester LE1 7GP

First edition November 1975
Reprinted 1976

ISBN 0 85110 580 7

Quotations from the Bible are from the
Revised Standard Version (copyrighted
1946 and 1952, second edition 1971, by
the Division of Christian Education,
National Council of the Churches of
Christ in the United States of America),
unless otherwise stated.

Printed in Great Britain by
Hazell Watson & Viney Ltd
Aylesbury, Bucks

Contents

5

Preface

This book is not a blueprint for Utopia. It would be folly as well as arrogance for any individual Christian to claim that he and he alone could interpret the Christian view of society. But there are broad principles for which Christians have stood over the centuries and especially since the church threw off so many alien influences in the sixteenth century. These principles are now being challenged as they have not been challenged for almost a thousand years. So Christians have to guard the foundations as they have never been guarded before.

First, many Christians have needed persuading that there is a Christian view of society. Ten or fifteen years ago this was a major task. The tradition of pietism and non-involvement was strong. There was a strong reaction against the 'social gospel' and a strong undercurrent of dispensationalism which taught that the world was beyond redemption until Christ's imminent return.

It has now been accepted that it is natural and right for the Christian to act as the salt of the earth as well as the light of the world. The danger now, perhaps, is that we may go in the opposite direction, believing that the Christian church must undertake a whole-hearted political commitment to introduce reform by any and every secular means. No sooner have Christians accepted that Wilberforce and Shaftesbury were in the mainstream of Christian tradition than we have complaints that they did not also work out a whole Christian political system, that they carried through their reforms only in an *ad hoc* manner without also reforming the system.

But the Christian must take a Christian view of human nature, not a Marxist view. Christ did not teach that the kingdom of heaven arrived through a change in the political system. He taught us to stand for certain principles, whatever the political system. Christianity is more concerned with ends than it is with means. It is pragmatic; 'By their fruits you shall know them.' The political system that is right for one country during one period of time may be quite wrong for another country and during another period of time. In many countries Christians are in a small minority with little immediate hope of changing the political system. In many they would be exterminated if they taught the view that a Christian was committed to end the political system and introduce another. This is one reason why it is neither wise nor kind of Christians in the democracies to urge Christian churches under totalitarian régimes to active political opposition. And in any case that is not the Christian way. The Christian way is to stand for the principles taught by Christ and the apostles. It is these principles that I have tried to outline in this book.

I have set out, first of all, the case for a moral order. The emerging order in formerly Christian countries is the 'permissive society'. But that is not a lasting order. It is based on a series of assumptions about human nature which are unproved and which most Christians believe to be quite wrong. It is likely, therefore, to fail and to produce a backlash which would be much harsher than any Christian moral order. So there is an urgent need to put the Christian case for a moral order. This I have tried to do in chapter 1.

The case for the permissive society does not simply say that society is adult and can do without a moral law. It actively opposes the beliefs which stand in its way. Some exponents of the idea, of course, go much further than others and it is not necessary to go into the differences between moderates and extremists to put the Christian alternative. This alternative is based first of all on the belief in the dignity of man who is made in the image of God. It is on this belief that our relations with our fellow men are founded. Every single person is entitled to respect. Wherever permissiveness undermines the dignity of the individual, we must oppose it. That is the subject of chapter 2.

The Christian believes not only that man was made in the image of God, but that all are sinners and that we need not only a moral law but also social institutions to help us to keep it. There are the divine institutions of family, church and state. All these institutions are currently under attack as outmoded and irrelevant, and I have devoted three chapters to try to show why they have never been needed more.

I have also included a chapter on 'The Nation'. Although government is a divine institution, it is no part of Christian teaching that the only legitimate government is one which corresponds exactly with a particular race. Ethnic nationalism has replaced Christianity as the religion of the twentieth century, and, because it appeals to the emotions and is apt to claim totalitarian loyalty as well, it is more dangerous than Marxism and certainly much more divisive.

We live in a materialistic society, and because so much public debate is about the way in which we organize our economic affairs, I have included a chapter on that too. We live in quite a new kind of society, one in which our scientific knowledge has far outrun our ability to agree on ways in which we should apply it. So we have far greater incomes than ever before, but far greater dependence on each other, making us all far more vulnerable to our mutual quarrels. Here, above all, we need to work out a mutually acceptable morality.

Finally I have come back to the permissive society, to contrast it in the last chapter with Christian liberty which is the only true freedom.

This book is not an academic treatise, bringing together all that every Christian and non-Christian author has written on the subject. It has been hammered out on the anvil of my own experience; it comes from attempts to translate Christian doctrine into practice as an industrial manager, a public servant, a deacon, a teacher of the young, a father, a husband and a friend. Its arguments have been sharpened by private and public discussions in Britain and overseas, some in the very public debate of radio and television.

Both academics and practical people have their contribution to make. The contribution of the academic is obvious. His sources are documented and can be checked. The experience of the practical person is not always worn on his sleeve. But it is none the less real. Those of us who have taken part in the crises of government, who have advised ministers in the confrontations between the power groups in society, develop a feel for the power structure and find out in real situations the power of particular beliefs and the effect they have on men's actions. Similarly those of us whose Christian service is with teenagers and students get a sense of the pressures of society on the young and trends in ideas which is more down to earth than those whose experience is secondhand. But an active life does not leave time to produce a book which is in any way comprehensive. I can only hope therefore that the reader will make due allowances.

I am most grateful to Dr Oliver Barclay for reading the first draft and for his extensive comments, and to Mr Ronald Inchley for all his help and advice – though I bear full responsibility for the final result. I would also like to thank my wife for all her most helpful comments and for her forbearance whilst the book was being written.

Balsham,
Easter, 1975

H.F.R.C.

1 The Christian moral order

Introduction

We live in an environment where the pace of change has left us dizzy and bewildered. The certainties of previous generations have been called in question and we are beginning to doubt the ability of human knowledge to understand or control the environment in which we live. 'Stop the world; I want to get off!' is the heartfelt cry.

As the rich countries try to corner essential natural resources we are told that already we have left only forty years' supply of oil and a few hundred years' supply of other vital raw materials. And because industrial power enables science to affect the balance of nature on a scale never known before, the world's ecology is under real threat.

Inflation, which used to be confined to certain countries where it seemed to be endemic, has spread to the more stable industrial democracies and has made it much more difficult for governments to control their economies. The traditional moral order has been upset by industrialization of rural economies and mass communication. The framework of authority has been upset by mass education which has called authority in question throughout the world. Then there has been a swing all over the world from religion to nationalism, which has taken its place as a kind of new religion— this seems to be an almost universal phenomenon associated with the end of imperialism and the adoption of the western non-religious attitude to life. There has been a change in the balance of international power between the rich nations and the poor, and the age-old scourge of famine has returned to plague large parts of the world.

At the same time the Christian has his own anxieties. The values of his faith, which have had some influence in the past, are now in decline. The non-religious attitude to life, despite the ideals of the humanists, seems to have opened the floodgates of materialism and sensuality, and all that Christianity has stood for now looks like so much flotsam in the flood. The Christian continues to argue his case, but the grounds of argument have been changed and he is put on the defensive. He is asked to prove by statistical correlation his belief that promiscuity, divorce by consent, pornography, homosexuality, euthanasia, soft drugs, violence on films and television and abolition of capital punishment will undermine the social fabric. This, not surprisingly, he feels incompetent to do. Not every Christian is a social scientist; yet many believe that the cumulative effect of all the changes in values, the increase in materialism and the decrease in self-restraint, will make it very difficult to maintain a civilized and humane society.

The Christian believes, nevertheless, that there ought to be a Christian answer to all the crises which affect society. He believes in a God who has laid down a relationship of human beings to their Creator, to each other and to the created universe. So there must be a Christian social order, to be applied by the ordinary Christian in the rough and tumble of an imperfect world. This social order, however, is idealistic, not repressive. It is opposed to what we may call the 'heresies of the right' which discount the common grace in man, discount his idealism and teach that man is not to be trusted and has to be held down. On the other hand, unlike the humanist, the Christian believes in sin. He recognizes that man requires the restraint of law and of custom. The 'heresies of the left' discount the sin in man and the need for such restraints. Christians must steer a middle road, believing both in sin and in common grace. People need ideals to work for and to live for: but they also need the re-straints of law and custom.

The Christian believes that these restraints should be based on the Christian moral code. We live in what is known as a permissive society, but we are now finding that permissiveness is indivisible. We cannot have permissiveness in sex and expect that we will not also have permissiveness in violence, or in tax avoidance, or in corruption and bribery in high places. People today want permissiveness in the bedroom, but not in the board room; in the casino, but not in the bank. If we promote permissiveness where we want it, we will find permissiveness where we do not want it. The Christian is in favour of promoting good order in society, which restrains the violence of the strong and persuades the rich to pay taxes to help the poor. He believes that without this good order and restraint the strong and rich will get stronger and richer, and the weak and poor will get weaker and poorer.

The nature of God and the created order

The Christian moral order starts with a belief in God as Creator. The argument about the existence of God is almost as old as human history. But it is a philosophical argument, not a scientific one. Some scientists are Christians and some are not. The only new ingredient today is the theory about origins which has gripped the public imagination as a convenient catch-all, explaining the physical universe without the need for God. The average person believes that this theory has been proved – or virtually proved – by exactly the same tests of experimental science as the discovery of penicillin or nuclear fission. But senior scientists will admit quite freely that, on the evidence of experimental science, the Christian is just as entitled to believe in creation as anyone else may believe in a universe which evolved without a creator. Both, they will say, are matters of faith.

There are also dangers in putting the mantle of the scientific method over metaphysical speculation. The founding fathers of the scientific method, such as Francis Bacon, confined the scientific method to what could be proved by experiment, separating decisively between science and speculation, between secondary causes which could be measured, systematized and rationalized, and primary causes which could not. They removed the physical sciences from arid speculation and studied 'the book of God's works' with the same fervour as they had studied 'the book of God's Word'. The scientific method can be deduced directly from 'the book of God's Word'. It is a study of secondary causes, based on what is revealed of the nature of the Creator.[1]

a. Unity in creation

The Christian believes first that the Creator is one.[2] There must therefore be unity in creation. The universe is not a chaos of conflicting laws created by a pantheon of fifty different gods. It is not an accidental and unrelated jumble with no rhyme or reason. It is not governed by fifty different 'space lords' or 'time lords' of science fiction. The laws of creation are a unified system; what is true in one part will be true in another. The God of the hills is also the God of the valleys; the God of the land is also the God of the sea. The pagan religions did not teach a unified structure of the universe because they did not believe in one God. Similarly the new superstitions of the new pagans do not reflect a belief in a unified universe. Anything may be going on 'out there' and, maybe, there are completely different rulers and completely different rules.

b. Love in creation

In the second place, the Christian believes that the Creator was a God of love,[3] that he made the universe for the benefit of mankind, that he has given us all that is needed to sustain us and that if people make the effort to unlock the secrets of nature they will find the treasure a good God has given them. The heavenly Father knows all our needs and he has provided for them.[4] This is a call to work and not to despair, a call to action, a feeling that the bounds of knowledge must be increased for the benefit of our fellows,[5] that the future lies in tapping the riches of a bountiful God rather than forcefully removing the possessions of our richer neighbours.

Since Christianity threw off its medieval cast of mind and relied more on the Bible and less on the Greeks, it has always had, as Professor Hooykaas has pointed out, this strong, activist, optimistic outlook.[6] This is in sharp contrast to other religions. It is no co-incidence that the scientific breakthrough took place in Christian countries and particularly in those countries whose faith was then closest to the teaching of the Bible and least influenced by other beliefs.[7] It is extremely difficult in a scientific age to think ourselves back into the presuppositions of those who did not know what we now know. They saw a nature which was harsh, cruel and arbitrary, and they supposed that the gods of nature must be harsh, cruel and arbitrary. It required a leap of faith far greater than we can now grasp to believe that God was good, that nature might be tamed, that what had been done here and there accidentally and haphazardly at long intervals might be done everywhere purposefully, systematically and much faster. People no longer dabbled in these things. They seized on them with enormous energy and in a few years made strides like those which had taken centuries before.

c. Order in creation

Thirdly, Christians believe that God is a God of order. The account of the creation is an account of the creation of order. Everything was created 'according to their kinds'.[8] Adam was told to catalogue the animals in creation.[9] The Mosaic law divides the animals by classes into those which are edible and those which are not.[10] The apostle Paul teaches that God is a God of order and not of confusion.[11] And if we examine the 'book of God's works' we shall find order. We can classify the creation into its different 'kinds'. The earth is not the confused scene which it appears to be. Everything has its place in the order and can be classified and described. This is contrary to the heathen view of the world which sees it as confused and disorderly.

d. A rational creation

Fourthly, the Christian believes in a God of reason. The Christian faith is therefore a reasoning faith. God spoke through Moses in reasonable language that plain people could understand.[12] The prophets reasoned with Judah and Israel. Christ continually reasoned not only with his disciples but also with those who opposed his teaching.[13] The apostles reasoned out the Christian faith in their great Letters – especially the apostle Paul with his massive intellect.

The universe of a rational God is therefore likely to be made by rational laws which can be discovered and understood by men. This belief encouraged the scientist to make the breakthrough from catalogues to systems, to discover the underlying principles which are common to whole classes of creation. As a result, instead of making cumbersome catalogues, he can simply note the marginal differences; and instead of the impossible task of finding the reaction of every part of creation to every other, he can discover the principles on which these reactions take place, the systems by which the reactions work. Once this body of experimental knowledge is built up, he can then test all new and unknown phenomena against the systems to find out where they fit and how they are likely to react. This is the heart of experimental science, and it rests on the belief in a rational creation.

Once the universe has proved to be rational, it is easy to think that this was obvious if only people had had the wit to see it. It would follow that the relationship which existed between religious belief and the discovery of a rational universe was only accidental and that such belief is no longer necessary now that the facts are known. But today belief in irrationality seems to be growing. It dominates the arts and it cannot be too long before it spills over into science. People will eventually act out what they believe; and if they no longer believe in rationality but in racial dominance or in the signs of the zodiac, then science will be affected too. Fewer people will take up science as a career. There will be hostility to the scientist and to his insistence on order and rationality, and scientific effort will become feebler as it loses the enthusiasm and energy which come from the support of society. The first signs of this may be appearing in a fall-off in the number of students wishing to study science at university level.

e. A stable creation and miracle

The fifth belief is that God's decrees are unchanging,[14] so that the scientific laws will be stable. One foundation of this belief is the explicit promise of God to Noah after the great flood that, from then until the end of time, there would be no further catastrophic breach in the natural laws; that seedtime and harvest, cold and heat, summer and winter, day and night, would not cease.[15] And throughout the Bible's account of God there are statements of his unchanging decrees. Unlike the assumptions about order and rationality, this assumption cannot be tested. The fact that laws have not changed during the short period of experimental science does not mean that they cannot change. Yet without this presupposition science is unthinkable. Enormous effort and energy go into cataloguing the natural order and discovering experimentally the systems by which it works. If this order is not stable, if the systems can be changed, then the effort and energy are not worth while. It required a strong belief in a stable universe to start the process; it requires a continuing belief to keep it going.

But how, it is often asked, does the Christian reconcile this scientific view of the world with the miracles recorded in the Bible? Do they have to be explained away? For those who accept that the world was created by God there should be no problem. If God made the natural laws, he can also change them. There can be no question that it is within the Creator's power to do so. The only question is whether it is the kind of thing a Creator would do. Why should the Maker of the universe interfere with the order which he has created? Why should he trouble to intervene on a particular day in a particular place?

A miracle always authenticates the person who performs it by giving him the ability, which can come only from the Creator, to change the order of nature. That is its purpose. It accepts that there is an order of nature, that it can be changed only by God, and that therefore the change in the natural order comes from God. Moses needed authentication from God if he was to bring Israel out of Egypt, if he was to persuade them to obey the law. Elijah and Elisha needed authentication if they were to make a wayward Israel come back to God. Gideon and Jonah needed to know that it was the voice of God which told them to take their lives in their hands. And the Jews were to be shown that Jesus was the authentic Messiah sent from God. The man who was born blind took the miracle of his sight as a sure sign of Christ's divinity.[16] The final taunt 'He saved others; he cannot save himself'[17] was turned on those who made it. It is just possible to believe that those who were healed might have recovered without him, but no-one except God could raise people from the dead and certainly no-one but God could himself rise from the dead. The resurrection was the climax to the authentication of Christ as the Son of God. The apostles were witnesses to the resurrection.[18] This was the pledge that all that he said was true. Their commission by the risen Christ was the basis of their authority.[19] But none of this undermines the stability of the natural laws. If there were no stability of natural laws, there would be no point in miracles because there would be no norm with which to contrast them.

f. Three great discontinuities

But this world, as we well know, is not perfect, and this suggests to many people the objection that, if God really made it, then he made it full of faults. 'What a beautiful world, Giles, the good Lord has made,' the clergyman in the old *Punch* cartoon is depicted as saying as he stood admiring his parishioner's garden. 'You should have seen the mess it was in when the Almighty had it on his own,' was the hard-working Giles' reply! But the Bible teaches plainly that God made the world perfect and that man, too, was created perfect and free. The fatal flaws appeared as man rebelled and disobeyed God's will. The first great discontinuity after the creation was this 'fall'. In some way, which we are not told about, the physical universe was changed. Man became subject to death[20] and the animals preyed on each other. Fear and dread entered the world.[21] Later there was a second dramatic discontinuity, a great natural catastrophe, sent by God in judgment,[22] and this also seems to have changed the physical laws at least to the extent of drastically shortening man's life on earth.[23] Both man's original rebellion and the two judgments of God on a rebellious world result in the mixture of good and evil which we find in the world today. There are, however, strong elements of continuity. Man may have to work by the sweat of his brow.[24] But he still retains the creative instinct of man made in the image of God the Creator. And he still retains his supremacy over the physical world.[25]

The third great event was the coming of Christ. This did not alter the physical laws. But it did alter the balance of good and evil, for it was a triumph of good and a conquest of evil. It inaugurated the kingdom of God, the kingdom of heaven, the kingdom of Christ.[26] It did not suspend the sentence of physical death, but it brought forgiveness and eternal life to all who believe and the promise of God's Spirit to each individual Christian. It inaugurated a universal church with a power to turn the world upside down. It fixed a terminal date to the power of evil and put it in chains until just before the end.[27]

The place of divine law

So we live in a world with a mixture of good and evil, right and wrong, in which the Christian church has the power to tilt the balance, to encourage good and to discourage evil. The church is now the custodian of God's law just as the Jews were before Christ. It has to teach the law to all who will hear and it has to put it into practice in the society in which it lives. This law is given by a good and loving God to help and to protect his creation. It tells his creatures how they should live together. It is the Maker's handbook, and those who observe it are likely to be happier than those who do not. The original sin was to question God's warning.[28] But he had loved those he warned, and, when they disobeyed, they found out that the warning was justified. The authority for God's law is his knowledge of us as our Creator. But he does not just know; he cares. Christ draws the parallel between the heavenly Father and the human father, whose children obey, not just because he is older and knows better, but because he loves and cares for them.[29]

Compare all this with the hostility of modern society to the idea of law. Is this opposition justified by what we know of human nature? Is the Christian view of the need for restraint so obviously wrong? Certainly no-one likes to be bound by laws. Everyone wants to feel free. But complete freedom is an illusion. Every society, if it is to survive, must have some kind of moral order, whether it is Christian, Marxist, Jewish or Muhammadan. Even the animist in the jungle has a moral order. There is a tendency in all men to do wrong, and society needs, therefore, to impose some kind of restraint.

The need for a moral order

There is a strong strand of thinking today which discounts the perversity in human nature. The theory is that society has come of age and has no further need for moralistic restraints. But if it is no longer obligatory to tell the truth, for example, how are people to know when they can trust each other?

In the past, two explanations of evil in society were popular. Some said the reason for it was poverty; people stole, for example, because they did not have enough to eat. Others argued that the cause was ignorance; people knew no better. If they were educated and lived in a civilized environment, evil would be banished. Such theories would lead us to expect, of course, the complete absence of wickedness in the upper classes of the day where there was plenty of money and education. Yet that is hardly what we find! But now this theory has been stood on its head and it is argued that it is an excess of affluence which causes all the evil! People have too much money and not enough to do.

The fact is that people are the same; human nature does not change. There is good and bad in both rich and poor; evil does not come from without, it is inside a person. The first British prime minister said cynically, 'All those men have their price.' Even if that is not strictly true, it is common knowledge that under extreme temptation people will do things which they would not do if the temptation were not there. Where law and order has broken down and there is no possibility of retribution, looting is the natural order. Where people are defenceless there is more cruelty. When shop-lifting is easy there is more of it; when it is made more difficult, it drops off.

Society needs a *personal morality* (the standards we set ourselves), a *social code* (the standards of behaviour we expect from each other without the need to go to law), and finally the *civil code* (which may be defined as what the great majority agree should be enforced by the law of the land). The case for the moral code is simply that no-one is wholly virtuous, that we all need standards of right and wrong. The case for civil law is that organized society needs a basis of stable relationships so that people who do not know each other can nevertheless trust each other, knowing that in the background there is a law which will be enforced.

The social policies of today rely heavily on the force of civil law to restrain the exploitation of the weak by the strong. Progressive taxation of income and heavy taxation of wealth are standard policies. So long as these taxes affect only a minority, and so long as the minority feel bound by strong standards of professional ser-vice, the implementation of such policies is possible. But as soon as redistribution spreads to the majority, the policies are in trouble. If shop stewards representing the higher-paid worker refuse to accept redistributive income policies, the drift of wealth to those with strong bargaining power from the workers with weak bargaining power, and the old and the feeble, is hard to stop. So we need some moral order to reinforce the law of the land if we are to have any redistribution from higher-paid to lower-paid.

On the other hand a moral order cannot be merely negative or repressive. There is still in most people something of the image of God, a conscience which responds to what is right and opposes what is wrong.[30] There is, in theological terms, a grace of God which is common to all mankind.

The doctrine of common grace is based on the teaching of God's love and patience. The world may be in rebellion, but God's Spirit is still at work. People were made 'in the image of God' and, how-ever rebellion may have spoilt this image, there is still a great deal that is noble in the human spirit. Mothers love their children; husbands love their wives; conscience is still very much alive; people can be horrified by evil and inspired by good. When the Christian church lives up to its standards, this side of human nature comes to the fore. When the church does not live up to its standards, when some perverse philosophy reigns, then people become cynical; and, in extreme cases, of which the Roman world at the beginning of the Empire is an example, God gives them over, as Paul tells us, to their own lusts.[31] But even then there are honourable men and women: the Ethiopian treasurer to Queen Candace,[32] the Roman centurion Cornelius,[33] Lydia, the Greek seller of purple,[34] all of whom seek something better. Even the Roman governor Felix, though he did not become a Christian, was affected by Paul.[35]

The Mosaic code: is it still valid?

The basis of the Christian moral code is the Ten Commandments. Christ summed these up in two great commandments, 'You shall love the Lord your God with all your heart, and with all your soul, and with all your strength, and with all your mind, and your neighbour as yourself.'[36] Even though the Ten Commandments were laid down by Moses for the children of Israel in mount Sinai, our Lord made it clear that they are still valid. He made it clear that he had come not to abolish the law but to fulfil it.[37] And although the moral law was codified by Moses, it was valid before him. Paul says of those who did not know the Mosaic law that they had the law in their hearts and used it as a standard by which to judge each other.[38]

There was a certain confusion in the early church about which parts of the Mosaic code were valid for the new Gentile Christians and which were not. And today there is a tendency to regard the whole Mosaic code as inapplicable to the Christian church and to sweep away the Ten Commandments with the ceremonial sacrifices and the sanitary laws of Moses' day. The Mosaic code certainly contained not only the Ten Commandments but also the ceremonial law of the Jewish church and the civil law of the Jewish nation. The ceremonial law came to an end at the death of Christ when the curtain in the temple, which cloaked the inner sanctuary or 'holy of holies', was torn from top to bottom, showing that the nature of God's relation with mankind had now changed.[39] And the civil law came to an end when the Jewish state finally ended in AD 70.

Christ drew the distinction between the moral and civil laws when he was asked about divorce. He said that the moral law forbade divorce, but that the civil law allowed it 'for your hardness of heart'.[40] No civil law, enforced by the state, can ever go as far as the moral law. The state can never set standards which are as high as people can set for themselves. If a law of divorce had not been allowed, women would still have been thrown out of their homes but would have had no legal standing. Divorce courts gave a woman a legally defined status and freed her from the obligations of a wife when she no longer had the privileges. But, as Christ pointed out, divorce was still morally wrong.

This also goes some way to explain the harshness of some of the penalties of the Mosaic civil code. A civil code can go only marginally beyond the circumstances of the time. The Israelites had, until then, been Egyptian slaves. They had no education, no separate civil order and, despite all the bondage of slavery, they still hankered after the certainties of Egypt. Their thinking was still dominated by Egyptian civilization and the life of the surrounding tribes. They lived right on the poverty level. There were no prisons in the desert. Corporal punishment and the death penalty were the normal punishments and if they were not judicially administered, it was evident from the law about cities of refuge[41] that the crimes committed would result in endless family and tribal feuds. It is clear that, in the very different conditions of Roman rule in the time of Christ, the Jews no longer punished by the Mosaic code.

But the Jewish civil code is still worth study, because we can deduce a good many principles from it which are more permanent than the actual laws. For instance, the code is a good deal tougher on offences against the person than it is on offences against property, whereas in our materialistic society offences against property now carry the greater sentences. In Britain in recent years we have had a longer prison sentence for robbing a mail train than for murder.

Again, the Jewish laws of jubilee were strongly redistributive.[42] The land, which was the principal means of livelihood, had to be redistributed every fifty years. It was an offence to add field to field, farm to farm, at the expense of less fortunate neighbours.[43] The laws against commercial exploitation were very strong. The laws of usury[44] prohibited neighbours from exploiting shortages by lending at rates of interest which could be met only by selling off land.

A great deal of emphasis is also given to laws protecting the family. Within the family there had to be complete trust and confidence. Sexual relations are strictly limited to husband and wife. The idea of sexual relationships of any kind between any other members of the family, or the husband or wife's family, must be completely absent. This did not include just the nuclear family but also the wider family of uncles, aunts, nephews, nieces, grandparents and grandchildren.[45] There must be confidence that the intimacy necessary for strong family relationships would never be abused, that a woman must never be disturbed by the risk of that kind of pressure in the security of her own home.

Slavery, that all-pervasive institution of ancient society, is severely limited.[46] The civil law evidently cannot abolish it altogether, but no Israelite must hold another Israelite as bondman for more than six years, after which he must be offered his freedom and given provisions to set up on his own. It is significant that we hear nothing more of slavery in the history of Israel.

The Mosaic civil code tells us that God had a certain order in creation and that his order must not be confused. He made men and women separate and the dress they wear must not hide the distinction.[47] He made men for women and women for men, and homosexual practices are against this divine order.[48] It was especially offensive to the divine order that humans should have sexual relationships with animals.[49] The divine order of nature was not an accident; it was created for our good and it was an offence to confuse it.

God created everything 'after his kind', and men and women with different functions and attributes. There is a functional balance which must not be upset. The tendency to equate women and men in every way upsets that balance. Men and women are equal before God, but they have functional differences in the family order and in the social order. To confuse them by treating the differences as though they did not exist is to throw a wholly unnecessary strain on the individuals, the family and society.

The Mosaic rules of evidence introduce another distinction between the moral law and the civil law. The civil law must have evidence.[50] Where evidence is impossible to come by, the law cannot operate. There can be a law against theft because theft can be proved. There can be no law against covetousness which is in the mind. It may lead on to theft, but until it does the civil law cannot act. There can be penalties against adultery, but not penalties against lust. And no civil law can force us to love God or our neighbour. The civil law can act only if our hate takes the form of attack or murder. The moral law is more comprehensive than the civil law and morally it is just as binding. But the judgment rests with God, not with the civil authorities.

The continuing need for a social code

Most civilized societies fill this gap between the jurisdiction of the civil law and the wider bounds of the moral law by a social code. Sometimes this is spelt out in the form of a professional code. Each of the great professions – the law, medicine, the public service – have detailed codes of behaviour to which their members are bound to conform. If members do not conform, they are warned or expelled from the profession. As a result the professions are generally trusted and accorded a high status in society.

Other codes operate more crudely and more informally. There is a code among those who lend and borrow huge sums of money and anyone who breaks it finds it difficult to get anyone to deal with him again. There is generally a greater trust in those who have some stake in society than in those who may disappear overnight. It used to be thought that only those who had a financial stake in society should be allowed any political power, but it was recognized eventually that other people, too, could be trusted with power. But if the bonds of civilized society were to be dissolved again and trust broke down, there might be pressure once more to limit power to those who had a stake to lose.

In this century there has been an enormous enlargement of social horizons as people started to trust each other on a far wider scale. As a result a narrow, suspicious climate has been replaced by far more generous behaviour. It is this openness and generosity which is put at risk as soon as the trust is abused.

The personal code: the Sermon on the Mount

Beyond the social code is the personal code, the standard someone sets for himself. It is into this category that we must put the Sermon on the Mount. Even a social code can go no higher than the society in which it operates. But a personal code can set entirely new standards. The Sermon on the Mount rises above legalism. It is generous. It does more, much more, than society expects. It goes the second mile; it gives and does not expect any reward.[51] And the effect, if it is practised to any purpose and on any scale, is to raise the standards of society far higher than they have ever been before. The righteousness of the Christian must exceed the righteousness of the scribes and Pharisees. It must show up not only the selfishness of sin, but the meanness of legalism. The Christian's social behaviour must remove all conceivable cause of criticism so that the only offence is the offence of the gospel he preaches, and so that even his enemies are put to shame.[52]

The Sermon on the Mount is not a new law; it is something altogether beyond the law, but a standard to which the Christian, through the help of the Holy Spirit, can attain. The moral order needs this spark of life. Dead orthodoxy is repressive,[53] and society needs inspiration far more than it needs repression. Man rebels against repression but rises to inspiration. It is this spirit of love which the Christian is meant to show. Maybe we can put down our enemies, but it is more effective to love them.

It is not easy to love our enemies. How is an apparently endless feud to be ended until one party or the other decides that they will forget? But no-one who has visited Ulster regularly during the shooting and bombing could imagine that civil order will be restored simply by the example of those who turn the other cheek. The national government has to provide a provincial constitution which enables the minority to take part in provincial government and to have some control over the forces of law and order. The major parties have to stand on a platform of compromise. The churches have to preach love and repudiate violence. The majority of the electorate have to give their votes to the parties of compromise. And finally, the tiny minority, who cannot impose their will except by bomb and bullet, have to be stopped. A moral order needs, therefore, those who will lead the way by turning the other cheek, and who will support the law and a stable moral order in which men can get on with each other. But it also needs a government which will impose the law on any small minority which insists on breaking it.

When order breaks down

Ulster shows the terrible problems which arise when a breakdown in moral order leads to a breakdown in civil order. As soon as order disappears, there is complete uncertainty and everyone's efforts and energies are directed to the protection of their immediate interests. Trust vanishes completely. Any stranger is a potential assassin. No-one dares oppose the actual assassins since he knows that he would be dead before help arrived. Old scores are paid off under the guise of political action. Business is carried on under constant demands for money for 'protection'. Friends dare not talk over the telephone and those in public positions live in constant fear for their lives. There is a stream of telephoned threats. Women live in fear for their husbands and children. Those who dismiss the need for moral order need a visit to west Belfast.

There may be those who think that, whereas some element of public morality is necessary, private morality ought to be left to the individual. But it is hard to see how they can be separated. If the authority of the family is destroyed, how are the youngsters on the streets to be brought to order? If society has said that teenagers can make up their own minds without reference to their parents, then they are entitled to shoot and bomb if they think it right without asking anyone's permission. And if parents cannot keep them under control, forces of law and order have to be far tougher in order to stop the violence.

Where permissiveness leads

Those whose main argument is for more permissive sexual morality may feel that their case has nothing to do with violence. But the freedom they want is not the liberty to make love – that has happened since the beginning of time. It is the freedom to abandon their partner, and that has been, through the centuries, a major cause of violence. Fathers and brothers have traditionally protected their daughters and sisters and have been dissuaded from doing so only when the law insisted on protecting them instead. History shows that the strong moral order of government was necessary to stop tribal feuds and the same strong, moral order was necessary to prevent violent feuding of families. It is up to those who want to remove society's protection of women to argue that private protection will not return – whether all the women want it or not.

The Christian is not being faced with an alternative moral order which has been tried in practice and whose results can be demonstrated. He is faced with a series of unproven assertions that this or the other part of the Christian moral order can be removed with complete safety, that the removal of a particular pillar will not bring the house down. There is nothing to prove, we are told, that a stable family unit is necessary; so promiscuity, adultery, homosexual practices and pornography are a matter of individual choice. There is nothing to prove that attacks on the 'establishment' will do anything but good, or that it does not really matter if the 'system' is brought down because every new society must first destroy the old. There is nothing to prove the connection between the permissive society and the rise in violent crime. After all, Cain killed Abel without any such provocation.

The Christian reply is that, if society is to be civilized, there must be a moral order which encourages the good in man and discourages the evil. Christianity is a balanced and cohesive moral order which is on the record and which has influenced all kinds of societies with greater or lesser success over nearly two thousand years. It has done a great deal to promote a free society because it encourages the maximum self-discipline which greatly reduces the need for imposed discipline. It is the alternative society and not Christianity that is unproven. While Christian influence remains, the attacks on our free and open society may not destroy it. But no-one knows when a social order dies, when the hope that all will come right in the end gives way to cynicism and fear. Confidence may take a long time to destroy, but, once dead, generations or even centuries may pass before it is renewed.

The oddity is that the people who treat the moral order so lightly are the very same ones who put the maximum demands on the power of the state to implement social change. If we are ever to break the backbone of poverty we need to switch vast sums of money from the rich to the poor. This can be done only if there is respect for the moral case and respect for the powers of government. There are many countries in which neither is respected and in which there is, as a result, an unbridgeable gap between rich and poor. If we are ever to abolish slums and have decent housing for all, then the local government which has to get the houses built needs to be uncorrupt. But permissiveness leads to financial corruption and financial corruption so destroys the relationships of trust on which government and business depend that housing programmes will never get off the ground. The moral order is indivisible. If attempts are made to destroy it, every part of it is vulnerable. If it is strengthened, one part will strengthen the other.

Our society needs the Christian moral order

A moral order gives a stable background to society. In a civilized society, the basic necessities of life can be taken for granted and men can get on with really constructive work. But once the stability of society is in doubt, no-one knows whether he can go on tomorrow with what he started today. Investment dries up, projects are postponed, all efforts and energies are directed to keeping the basic functions in being. So all that is progressive and all reforms are first shelved and then forgotten. A civilized society needs a stable base, and a stable base needs an agreed moral order.

Each moral order the world has known is different, but the Christian one probably contains the greatest element of personal freedom. Since the individual is directly answerable to God, the Christian order rests to the maximum extent on individual personal responsibility and as little as possible on the sanctions of society and state. It does not need the element of brutal repression which so many other moralities mete out to non-conformists. Of course, great brutalities have been carried out by principalities and powers using the name of Christianity to put down their political enemies. But since these actions have been quite counter to its teaching, the true teaching has, in the end, reasserted itself and the brutalities have been repudiated as having no part in the Christian message.

The power of the Christian moral order rests on its appeal to men's consciences. It is an innate power rather than an external power. And it is a power which is greatly reinforced by the example of a practising Christian church. That is what Christ meant when he said that the church was to be the salt of the earth and the light of the world. The salt is to prevent corruption. The light is to illuminate the truth, to inspire men and women to a better life.

Notes

1. See the quotations from Christopher Hill's *Intellectual Origins of the English Revolution* (Oxford University Press, 1965) and Professor Sir Herbert Butterfield's *The Origins of Modern Science 1300–1800*[2] (Bell, 1957) in the Appendix to my *The Christian in Industrial Society*[2] (Inter-Varsity Press, 1966), pp. 114–26. Another useful work is *Religion and the Rise of Modern Science* (Scottish Academic Press, 1972) by R. Hooykaas, Professor in the History of Science in the University of Utrecht. The distinctions which Professor Hooykaas makes between the pagan, Greek, Catholic and Protestant views of science are especially interesting. For a summary of his argument see Appendix A, pp. 33ff.

2. See Deuteronomy 6:4.   3. 1 John 4:8.

4. In Matthew 6:31ff. Christ promises that God will clothe and feed the faithful. *Cf.* Matthew 5:45: 'Your Father who is in heaven . . . makes his sun rise on the evil and on the good, and sends rain on the just and on the unjust.'

5. The Christian believes that everyone has God-given talents which he must improve and increase. See Matthew 25:14–30; Luke 19:11–27.

6. See Appendix A, pp. 33ff.

7. See the Appendix on the Weber-Tawney thesis in my *The Christian in Industrial Society*.

8. See the repeated use of this expression in Genesis 1.

9. Genesis 2:19f.   10. Leviticus 11.   11. 1 Corinthians 14:33.

12. For example, the Ten Commandments have been passed down from generation to generation over thousands of years and have been accepted as a base for the social and civil codes in all kinds of different societies.

13. See, for example, Matthew 22:15–46, where Jesus reasons with both Pharisees and Sadducees, and the incident ends, 'And no one was able to answer him a word, nor from that day did any one dare to ask him any more questions.'

14. *Cf.* Malachi 3:6, 'I the Lord do not change.'

15. Genesis 8:22. It is only at this point, after the catastrophe of the flood, that this promise of stable natural laws is made. According to the Old Testament account there had been changes in natural laws not only at the flood, but at the fall. The Christian believes in stable natural laws since then, but in my view this provides no basis for the extrapolation of all the present natural laws through the flood back to creation. In any case the Christian is not bound to believe that the laws by which the universe was created are the same as those by which it has been sustained before or since the flood.

16. John 9.   17. Matthew 27:42; Mark 15:31; Luke 23:35.

18. Acts 2:32. Paul was not an apostle at the time of the resurrection and explains his witness to the resurrection in 1 Corinthians 15:7f.: 'Then he [Christ] appeared to James, then to all the apostles. Last of all, as to one untimely born, he appeared also to me.'

19. Acts 1:1–8.   20. Genesis 2:17.

21. Genesis 9:2.   22. Genesis 6:5–8.

23. Genesis 6:3. Compare this life-span of the patriarchs with the much longer lives of the antediluvians and the even shorter life-span later. The first appearance of the rainbow seems to show that the vapour covering of the earth was not the same before and after the flood.

24. Genesis 3:19.   25. Genesis 9:2.

26. These are the names given by Christ to the church age, which started with his ministry on earth and continues through the ministry of the Holy Spirit.

27. Matthew 28:18: 'And Jesus came and said to them, "All authority in heaven and on earth has been given to me." ' He then commissioned the apostles to preach with his authority to all nations. Note also 1 Corinthians 15:25, 'For he must reign until he has put all his enemies under his feet'; John 12:31, 'Now is the judgment of this world, now shall the ruler of this world be cast out'; John 16:11, 'The ruler of this world is judged'; Revelation 20:1–3, 'Then I saw an angel coming down from heaven, holding in his hand the key of the bottomless pit and a great chain. And he seized the dragon, that ancient serpent, who is the Devil and Satan, and bound him for a thousand years, and threw him into the pit, and shut it and sealed it over him, that he should deceive the nations no more, till the thousand years were ended. After that he must be loosed for a little while.' It seems to me that these four passages must be taken together and that if we do this, it is impossible to maintain that Revelation 20:1–3 does not apply to us, but only to some future dispensation. The effect of this dispensational teaching is to weaken the belief in the present power of Christ. Since the teaching spread we have looked to our own devices to revive Christian power, not to its Author.

28. Genesis 3:1, 'Did God say?'   29. Matthew 6:32.

30. Romans 2, summed up in verse 15, 'They show that what the law requires is written on their hearts, while their conscience also bears witness.'

31. Romans 1:24.

32. Acts 8:27ff. The Ethiopian had 'come to Jerusalem to worship' and 'was reading the prophet Isaiah'.

33. Acts 10:1ff. Cornelius was 'a devout man who feared God with all his household, gave alms liberally to the people, and prayed constantly to God'.

34. Acts 16:14. Lydia was 'a worshipper of God'.

35. Acts 24:25. 'Felix was alarmed' (AV, 'trembled').

36. Luke 10:27. (See also Mark 12:30, 31 and Matthew 22:37.)

37. Matthew 5:17.

38. See note 30 above and Romans 2:1, 'Therefore you have no excuse, O man, whoever you are, when you judge another; for in passing judgment upon him you condemn yourself, because you, the judge, are doing the very same things.'

39. Matthew 27:50f.

40. Matthew 19:8; Mark 10:5f. 'For your hardness of heart Moses allowed you to divorce your wives, but from the beginning it was not so.'

41. Numbers 35:9–34.   42. Leviticus 25:10–34.

43. Isaiah 5:8: 'Woe to those who join house to house, who add field to field, until there is no more room.'

44. Leviticus 25:35–38.

45. Leviticus 18:6–18. This law was broken by David's son Amnon, who took advantage of the dutiful care of his half-sister Tamar to rape her, causing chaos in David's family which was never repaired. See 2 Samuel 13.

46. Leviticus 25:39–46; Exodus 21:1–6; Deuteronomy 15:12–18.

47. Deuteronomy 22:5.   48. Leviticus 18:22.   49. Leviticus 18:23.

50. Deuteronomy 17:6; 19:15. The 'two or three witnesses' of the Jewish law were demanded by Paul in 2 Corinthians 13:1. At Christ's trial before the Sanhedrin the witnesses could not be got to agree (see Mark 14:55ff.). Finally, after Jesus had said that he was the Christ, the high priest asked, 'Why do we still need witnesses?' (verse 63).

51. Matthew 5:41f.

52. Proverbs 16:7: 'When a man's ways please the Lord, he makes even his enemies to be at peace with him.' *Cf.* 1 Peter 2:15, 'For it is God's will that by doing right you should put to silence the ignorance of foolish men.'

53. The orthodoxy of the Pharisees and scribes was condemned by Christ on these grounds. See, for example, Matthew 23:4: 'They bind heavy burdens, hard to bear, and lay them on men's shoulders; but they themselves will not move them with their finger'; and *cf.* James 2:26: 'For as the body apart from the spirit is dead, so faith apart from works is dead.'

Appendix A: Different views of science

In his book *Religion and the Rise of Modern Science* (see note 1, p. 30) Professor R. Hooykaas contrasts the pagan, Greek, Catholic and Protestant views of science as follows.

In the Christian view, 'in total contradiction to pagan religion, nature is not a deity to be feared and worshipped, but a work of God to be admired, studied and managed. In the Bible God and nature are no longer both opposed to man, but God and man together confront nature. The denial that God coincides with nature implies the denial that nature is god-like' (p. 9).

The Greeks saw nature as 'a living divine organism, producing all things, all gods, men and animals, by generation' (p. 9). This idea of nature as a 'semi-independent power' was continued in the middle ages, such was the reverence for Greek philosophy in the Christian church. 'When things happened according to nature, this meant that they followed a pattern that seemed rational to the human mind, one which had been discovered by Aristotle ... In the middle ages, then, the biblical view was only superimposed on, and did not overcome, the Aristotelian conception' (p. 12).

The medieval view was challenged at the Reformation. 'A more fully biblical world view has, since the sixteenth century, favoured the rise in modern science' (p. 13). Aristotle was based on reason, but Christianity was based on experience, however unreasonable. 'The apostles proclaimed, not those things which seemed reasonable to them, but those things which "they had seen with their eyes and their hands had handled". This, transferred to the field of science, means that, just as the faith of the Christians was founded not on a cleverly excogitated system, but on what they recognized to be the hard facts, so science has to accept facts, even when they seem to be against reason and rule' (p. 30).

The first break came with Kepler and Galileo. 'Kepler ... submitted to given facts rather than maintaining an age-old prejudice; in his mind a Christian empiricism gained the victory over platonic rationalism' (p. 36).

In the seventeenth century, Boyle 'pointed out that both science and religion are based on fundamentals that are incomprehensible, and that both are founded on facts historical rather than rationally cogent'. The philosopher 'thinks that he understands all things and that nothing which does not conform to his philosophy could be true'. But 'empirical science is an ally of religion ... hostility exists only between speculative metaphysics on the one side and religion cum true science on the other' (p. 48).

The return to the Bible also liberated technology. 'Whereas the Greeks felt that to command nature was to attempt the impossible ... the biblical authors believed that God has conferred some of his divine power of command on the highest of his creatures' (p. 63). 'Francis Bacon, the herald of modern science, defended this view ... "Many have not only considered it to be impossible but also as something impious to try to efface the bounds nature seems to put to her works." In Bacon's opinion God has made us his fellow-workers and given us the commandment to investigate his works' (p. 68).

'Francis Bacon pointed out how hard was the labour of the vast majority of men, and how poorly they could feed and clothe themselves in spite of all their efforts. He blew the trumpet in the war against the sins of laziness, despair, pride and ignorance and he urged his contemporaries, for the sake of God and their neighbours, to reassume the rights that God had given them and to restore that dominion over nature which God had allotted to man.' 'Thus modern technology, that is, technology closely connected with science, found its most eloquent advocate in a man who placed it on a decidedly Christian basis' (pp. 71, 72).

2 The dignity of man

All men are equal

At the heart of the Christian moral order is the Christian teaching about man. It tells us that we are made in the image of God the Creator, that the image is spoilt through man's rebellion against God, that nevertheless God's grace still operates in man, that everyone is redeemable,[1] that their lives can be transformed,[2] that God knows and cares for each man, woman and child,[3] that however hardened someone's conscience, however much his fellows may despair of him, God is still patient.[4] If each human life is of such immense significance to the God who made us, the life of each human being should be of significance to all his fellow humans. Man is not an animal; he has been placed in charge of all the natural creation and he has an eternal soul which is redeemable, and, once redeemed, will never perish.[5] The thief on the Roman cross of execution was welcomed by Christ into Paradise.[6] Rahab the harlot was welcomed, not only into the line of faith,[7] but into the ancestry of Christ.[8] The Samaritan woman, who had gone through five husbands and was living as a man's mistress shunned by her neighbours, brought all the town out to the feet of Christ.[9] Many Christians know of the most brutal characters who, when they became Christians, were transformed into people full of natural dignity who help and encourage all around them.

Christ took notice of everyone. He ate with the common people[10] and with the Pharisees.[11] All of them were significant.

The Christian church is open-ended, not closed. There cannot be too final a distinction between those within the church and those outside it. The man who persecuted the church on the way to Damascus was a Christian when he got there.[12] The person who is a pagan today may be a Christian tomorrow. Peter told the Christians to behave so that no-one could possibly have any grievance against them.[13] To tell people that they needed to repent and that their own good deeds were not enough to save them was quite enough to give offence without adding to it! Christians must have no part in the wrongs that people do or in the attitude of mind that leads to those wrongs, but they must have a care for all who do them. Paul tells us that, although immorality and worldliness are to be avoided within the church, this does not mean that we must cut ourselves off from all contact with immoral and worldly people outside it.[14] So the Christian faith respects the dignity of every individual, however apparently alien or hostile, however far removed from the image of God. No-one is to be written off, no-one put outside the bounds of care and compassion.

The importance of education

The Christian view of the dignity of man has led Christians to be the strongest promoters of education. Christ taught, in the parable of the pounds and the parable of the talents[15] – the repetition of a truth is his way of underlining it – that God has given everyone talents, that it is our positive duty to multiply these talents, and it is a sin to be strongly condemned if we do not. No doubt the parable applies to spiritual talents, but there is no reason to exclude any kind of talent. Education has a key role in the whole of this process.

Countries with the strongest Christian ethic have always put great emphasis on education, have always believed that man made in the image of God should be able to develop all his faculties to the full. This is not a natural view. The natural attitude towards uneducated people is that they are incapable of having their minds improved, and there has also been strong opposition by ruling élites on the grounds that too much education is politically dangerous.

But the idea that we must develop the human mind and personality to the full has prevailed. The danger in education, as in everything else, is that it may become separated from its moral base. It then becomes a technical process unrelated to a view of life, unrestrained by any limit on the use to which the new knowledge should be applied.

Man is not a machine

If man is made in the image of God, he will have, however deeply buried, some of the creative character of God. There is an instinct in each of us to do something worth while. Even as children we want to make things. Each of us wants to leave behind something to mark our passage through life. In some people, of course, this instinct is fairly well suppressed. Indeed, there are those in whom the image of God is so spoiled that they seem to get more pleasure from destruction than from creation. But those who have to organize the work of others know that there is an instinct there which they ignore at their peril. While mankind is on the poverty line, survival is the first instinct. We have to live; and if dull, back-breaking work enables us to live, we put up with it, not thinking much beyond the next meal. Yet even in subsistence economies those who are close to the land can see the fruit of their labours.

But when work is organized on a grand scale and sub-divided, each individual's job can easily become a meaningless part of the whole where few ever see the finished product at the end of the line. Work becomes dehumanized and man becomes no more than a fractional-horsepower engine with a cheap control mechanism. His instinct tells him that he was meant to be more than this and he becomes dissatisfied. Not surprisingly, therefore, the statistics show that people with boring, routine tasks tend to move on restlessly from one job to another, and that people engaged in creative work tend to stay in their jobs much longer. There is more stability, for instance, among garage mechanics, to whom every repair is different, who meet the customer, who see the whole job through, who have the satisfaction of putting a faulty car on the road again, than there is on the motor-production line where the whole job has been de-skilled and where the machine, in the form of the line, dominates the man who does nothing but turn a nut with a spanner every hour of every day of every week of every year. There have been a number of studies of production lines which have told the car companies to build the skill back into the job and to restyle the job so that a man will build a car which is his car.

One of the chief engineers of a Swedish company, building a new plant on this basis, was asked whether it was not more expensive. He said it depended on how you calculated the expense. At present very few Swedes were prepared to work on a vehicle-production line and the companies had to depend on immigrant labour. Absenteeism was high. When the production line was in operation it was a bit cheaper; but they wanted to go on building vehicles and felt that their next plant had to be one which workers would be prepared to operate.

As a general rule women are more tolerant of routine than men. In offices they may be found cheerfully doing routine jobs, such as punching computer cards, which a man would find endlessly boring. Many women still see bringing up a family as the most creative part of their life and their job outside the home is not the central thing. But that is not true of all women and the famous Hawthorne experiments carried out in the United States in the thirties showed that they can respond strongly when their job is made more significant.[16] The experiment started by an improvement in the lighting to make conditions more tolerable. Output went up and continued to go up over a series of experiments. Then, on some instinct, the experimenters reversed part of the process, making the lighting worse. Output still went up. A similar series of experiments showed the same pattern. The conclusion was that personal attitudes mattered far more than physical conditions. The bosses were interested in what they did and, for the first time, their jobs had taken on real significance.

There is now, in most industrial societies, a drift away from manual work to jobs with a higher degree of professional skill. The trend is to avoid giving people work to do which can be done by machines. An increasing number spend their time in designing and in programming machines. More time is spent, too, in service industry of all kinds and the services are more highly skilled and more professional. Universities and other colleges of higher education have been expanding vigorously. The professional is not always paid more than the manual worker, but very few of them would want to change just for the money. The element of creativity in professional work is too strong a pull. Few people, for example, write books just for the money. But the creative element in writing is very strong and, although the financial rewards are poor, there is an endless supply of writers. All of this seems to reflect the truth of the Christian view of man as a creative being.

The demand for freedom

God the Creator is free, bound only by his own moral nature. There is also in man this instinct that he should be free, that only in freedom can he be truly creative and fulfil the potential of his own personality. Anyone who has ever been in charge of the work of creative staff knows the need to allow them the maximum freedom if they are to make the maximum contribution. This demand for creative freedom can be abused, of course, but the underlying need is genuine. Big business, for instance, cannot be run successfully as an autocracy. Henry Ford nearly wrecked the business he had built up by trying to run it all himself. Most major companies have long had a policy of decentralization so that middle management can use its own initiative to the maximum. Analysis of political autocracies shows that they are not efficient. No one person, no small group of people, can possibly know all the answers. Comparison of the war efforts of Germany in 1939–45 with those of Britain, for example, showed that the British developed a far more intense war effort than the dictatorship and that German leadership made appalling blunders because there was no critical check on its mistakes. But the myth of the efficient dictatorship dies hard. Despite all evidence to the contrary it is generally believed that dictatorship is more effective in controlling inflation.

On the other hand, freedom cannot operate without a firm framework. God is bound by his nature to be good, to be patient, to be just, to be holy. He cannot do anything which denies his own nature. So man made in the image of God must use his freedom in a similar framework. Anything else produces chaos, freedom for one at the expense of bondage for another. So sin creates bondage in which we cannot be free. Christ said, 'No-one can serve two masters';[17] and he promised that those who served him would be 'free indeed'.[18] This is the experience of all Christians. Lawlessness – which obtains its freedom at the expense of someone else – creates the backlash of oppression in which no-one is free. It is the inner code, the self-discipline, which creates real freedom.

Race and class

In a world divided by material suspicion people tend to group together for protection. The Christian's regard for his fellows must cross all these barriers.

All people are made in the image of God – Jews and Arabs, black and white, Celt and Scot, Czech and Slovak, Indian and Pakistani, Chinese and Japanese, Ibo and Hausa, German and Slav, Flem and Walloon, Croat and Serb, Afrikaans and Bantu. There is no basis whatever in Christian teaching for the belief that one race is in any way intrinsically superior to another. Some have had enormous advantages, not least of which is the tradition of a Christian social order. Others have had all kinds of problems. But all people are made in the image of God and all require respect. It is wrong, therefore, to treat whole races as sub-human, nothing more than a higher class of animal.[19]

Christian respect must also cross all barriers of class. The language of class warfare is just as objectionable as the language of racial warfare, and in some ways more objectionable just because it is so artificial. Why should we classify ourselves into upper, middle and lower classes? The classification has no useful function, but it has the malignant effect of dividing people who do not need to be divided. Whatever difference does it make to a man's character whether he wears tweeds or flannel, a tie or an open neck, whether he speaks with one accent or another? In England, a Welsh accent indicates a worker, but a Scottish accent may not. So many educated politicians painfully observe the shibboleths of accent to show that they are genuinely working class. At the other extreme books have been written which enable the readers to distinguish the accents of the 'genuine' upper class. Never mind that someone hasn't two wits to put together; if he pronounces the 'au' in 'Austrian' as the 'aw' in 'awful', he is upper class. If he pronounces it like the 'o' in 'ostrich', he is not. But the 'worker' is not someone who works for a living – nothing so simple. He must work with his hands. But a surgeon is not a genuine 'worker' even though he wears overalls and a cap, because his knowledge is more important than his manual dexterity. Nor is it a matter of union membership. Half or more of manual workers in most industrial countries are not members of trades unions. And it is doubtful whether airline pilots, who are members, would qualify, because on the aircraft they hold positions of command.

The apostle James tells the churches that they must not pay the slightest regard to signs of social class – they must not be partial between one member of the church and another.[20]

Dignity and degradation

The Christian respect for the dignity of man includes an especial respect for the dignity of woman. Many societies have treated women first as playthings, then as drudges; but they are created equal by God, they are responsible to God, they have soul and spirit, and in Christ there is 'neither male nor female'.[21] They have a separate role in the church, the family and in society, which is set out in both the Old and New Testaments. They have special obligations and special privileges. Their dignity should not be removed by pornography, or by social pressures which make them vulnerable to exploitation.

It is also an offence to degrade a man. All who are made in the image of God are entitled to their dignity, to respect from their fellows, and this must not be removed. To despise a man is to remove his dignity from him in our own mind. To treat him as a fool is to turn the inner thought into an outward attitude. It is wrong to remove the regard of other people for someone by gossip and slander. It is wrong to take away someone else's dignity by making them drunk. Parents should never make their children look ridiculous in public. Husbands and wives should not make fools of each other. A superior should always allow his subordinate to maintain his dignity.

The belief that we are made in the image of God also lies behind the Christian's natural reluctance to lose control of himself, through drink, through drugs or even through temper.[22] It is not just that someone incapable of controlling himself may be a danger to others; it is also degrading. Man was not meant to live on that level.

The most extreme way of degrading a fellow human being is violence. The Mosaic civil code treats violence against the person as a major crime. It is hardly surprising that the decline in Christian belief has been followed by a sharp rise in violence and the use of torture. The active practice of violence may be confined to a minority, but the increase reflects a broader attitude in society where a young man can balance a man's life against the contents of his pocketbook.[23]

Capital punishment for murder

The crime with the highest penalty in most civil codes is murder. Until very recently the penalty for murder in most countries was death. Since the Jewish civil code had the death penalty for a number of offences, for all of which it has long since been abolished in Christian countries, many Christians do not feel that there is any special reason why it should not be abolished for murder too. We have agreed that the Old Testament Jewish civil code is not binding on the Christian. But the principle is spelt out also in the covenant between God and Noah, under which God undertook that never again should there be a flood to destroy the earth. The covenant requires from man that 'of every man's brother I will require the life of man. Whoever sheds the blood of man, by man shall his blood be shed; for God made man in his own image.'[24] The crime of taking the life of man made in the image of God is so terrible that the man who commits it has forfeited the right to live. Indeed society must not let him live.

Those who dismiss the Old Testament will, of course, dismiss this covenant with Noah. But Christ endorses the Old Testament.[25] Peter refers to the days of Noah.[26] When Paul wants to establish a point about salvation by faith he refers back to Abraham.[27] The writer to the Hebrews, wanting to make clear that Christ's priesthood did not depend on the Mosaic law, went back to Melchizedek.[28]

We cannot separate the two Testaments, nor can we treat the earlier part of the Old Testament as inferior to the later part. The creation ordinances are vital. God's promise in covenant to Noah still holds. In writing to the Romans, Paul says of the civil authority, 'He does not bear the sword in vain.'[29] It can be argued that the sword is merely symbolic. But then why is the sword the symbol? Surely because the civil power is entitled to use the sword. Capital punishment is not judicial murder. God who gave life is entitled to take it again, and he has delegated this power to the state whenever it is proved that one man has wilfully taken the life of another.

The death penalty is a very emotive issue. Man was not originally made to die and any death is an awesome event. But what is in question is whether someone who has taken another person's life ought to be allowed to keep his own life.

The Bible takes us away from the murderer and back to the victim. Today we tend to forget the victim on the grounds that we can do nothing about the dead; the event is past and there is nothing more to be done. But in any terrible event there is always something more to be done. If there is an air disaster, or a terrible epidemic of cholera, or a famine, we do not take the view that the event is over, that the dead are dead and there is nothing more that can be done. The sheer number of deaths makes its impact. But, to God, one murder of a human being made in his image is terrible and cannot

44

be allowed to stand. To take a life which God has given is a terrible act and requires an awesome punishment. There is, God says, only one punishment fit for that crime.

The argument about deterrence is based on expediency. The Christian argument must be based on principle. A military commander may decide, as a deterrent, to shoot one captured guerrilla in ten and if that is not effective one in five. If he found that one in four was the effective level, would we approve? I doubt it. To argue with statistics on levels of deterrence may be all right on other crimes. On murder we need to decide whether capital punishment is right or wrong in principle.

The Christian looks beyond death. The humanist, however, sees it as the end of everything. He must therefore oppose the death sentence for he has nothing to say to the condemned murderer, no advice to give, no hope to offer. He cannot ask God to have mercy on the murderer's soul. Any life in being must be preserved at all costs for without life there is nothing.

The question comes back to one of authority. God our Maker has told us that human society cannot tolerate murderers. Because of the antibodies of conscience, and the divinely ordained institutions of family, state and church, it can tolerate a good deal of evil. But to tolerate murderers living among them is beyond the power of the antibodies in the social order God has given. The system cannot stomach it. It has to get rid of the poison or the whole system will be poisoned. It is a painful and sometimes alarming business to get rid of poisons, but it has to be done. The humanists say that this has yet to be proved. But how do you prove that poison is fatal to the system? In the end you can prove it only by dying.

The case for capital punishment can be argued even by those who do not accept the authority of the Bible. Murder is the tip of the whole dangerous iceberg of violence. Once the ultimate punishment is removed the violent man no longer has to be careful about the precise effect of his violence. Sometimes, indeed, if his victim dies, he is less likely to be caught. Then violence is used in robbery where it was not used before; robbing becomes more successful; crime begins to pay. Money is available to corrupt the forces of the law

45

and as soon as the citizen cannot trust the law, he begins to protect himself. The next step – one already taken in Northern Ireland – is the blood feud. It is the use of the wider family for protection where the state is incapable or unwilling.

This is not an outlandish scenario. The typical 'Western' film turns on the attempt to impose the law of the land in the place of the family feud. The feud is wrong because 'Vengeance is mine, I will repay, says the Lord',[30] and 'every person' is to 'be subject to the governing authorities'.[31] But when you talk to people in Belfast who have looked down the wrong end of a gun barrel, and to people who know that those who killed their fathers, mothers, brothers and sisters are alive and walking the streets, you can understand why this protective sub-culture comes into being.

The sting of death

Man made in the image of God was not originally meant for death; he was meant for eternal life. Death is not just the final non-functioning of a physical system, the falling of an autumn leaf, a small incidental part of the long evolution of a species, an atomic part of a cosmic process. Each human death is a tragedy, a black necessity caused by sin. The sign of man's rebellion is death, the end of the physical body of rebellious man which could never come into the presence of a just and holy God.

The passage of a human soul from time to eternity is an occasion for silent wonder. When someone leaves his human body to face his Maker, he acquires a certain dignity. He is a soul who must answer alone before God without the trappings of a family, race, poverty or wealth.

The man of the world may say that the Christian notions of eternal life are no more than wishful thinking. We do not want to die so we invent eternity. But why do we not want to die? What instinct in us feels that death is all wrong, that we were not meant to grow old and die, but to remain young and live for ever? Why do we have this obsession with eternal youth, this impatience with age and dread of death? If death is a part and parcel of the natural process, why do we feel so bad about it? Surely we should welcome it; but we do not. We regard it as a tragedy because it *is* a tragedy. And we feel that it is inconceivable that the human spirit should finally be extinguished, because it is true – it will not finally be extinguished. When a great and lively character dies, we find it hard to believe that someone so full of life should have gone for ever. We half expect his head to come round the door with a few caustic comments on the current scene. There have been companies where the executives dared not move the furniture out of the office of their late chairman. Daphne du Maurier's Rebecca lived on in Manderley to confound the second Mrs de Winter. A few miles north of Carmarthen, on the road to Cardigan, is a large country house with one first-floor window permanently blinded, the room of a son who was killed in the First World War. They will not come back, but our every instinct, our natural primitive awareness of the truth, tells us that their spirit is not finally quenched. That is also the Christian message, and it agrees far more with our deepest convictions than the harsh doctrine that death is natural and oblivion is final.

Suicide and euthanasia

It is not surprising that as Christian belief declines, self-inflicted violence is increasingly tolerated and excused. For without God there is no hope. The humanist outlook is eventually hopeless, and not every humanist can be a stoic. If we are nothing but a body, then, when physical and mental stress become intolerable, we are driven to feel that we must put an end to them. And once suicide becomes a possibility, it constantly presents itself to the mind and creates its own stress. Nor is it any wonder that, when the great stabilizers in society – the family, the state, the church – are weakening and coming apart, the stresses on the individual seem too great for him to bear in his loneliness. God said 'It is not good that the man should be alone'.[32] Twentieth-century urban man and woman have decided that this is not proved. They may not aim to live alone but they are less and less inclined to make the compromises and concessions needed for living with each other. And as people live increasingly for themselves, they not only begin to live alone but can become isolated and withdrawn, living their own life even in the company of others. But we were not meant to be alone, and in those tempted to suicide the balance of human companionship is not there to stop them. The suicide looks at his own problem. Companionship forces you to look at other people's problems. Of course, married people commit suicide, too, and churches cannot always prevent unbalanced members from committing suicide. But they certainly try to do so; and one cannot but believe that endless patience, understanding, willingness to listen, human company and genuine Christian love are successful in making the suicide of a professing Christian a very rare event. Indeed, the hope of the Christian makes this gesture of despair meaningless, and even if he is tempted, he knows that only God is entitled to take the life he gave him and that, until that time comes, God has work for him to do.

We tend today to have little use for the old, and arguments are being put forward for taking the life of the chronically sick and suffering to relieve them of their misery. But some of the very old and very frail can be a tremendous inspiration. Their determination in disability, their cheerfulness in the shadow of death, their thoughtfulness for others, their interest in all the people around them give those of us with lesser problems some sense of proportion. Age, weakness and death dramatize visually the tragedy of man originally made in the image of God eternal. But age can show up the spiritual character of man's nature in contrast. As the body dies, the spirit can often burn brighter. The Christian life is compared to the refining furnace.[33] The metal which has gone through the furnace has lost its dross, and the spirit which has endured all life's trials has a quality not obtainable in youth. In the Christian social order, age has a unique contribution to make in accumulated wisdom, in developed character and in unquenchable spirit.

The non-religious view of man

The intellectual opposition to the Christian view of man comes from the humanist. But since many of his values come from Christianity, there is much that is Christian in the humanist view of man. The humanist sees the good in human nature, though he tends to discount the evil. He believes in the dignity of man and woman and can protest about pornography quite as vigorously as the Christian. But in removing man's belief in God, he has also removed man's belief in man made in the image of God. And the common view of man is now quite different from that of the thoughtful and well-meaning humanist. The real belief of the average person appears in what he does rather than in what he says. But above all it appears in the arts.

Art reveals what people will not say; it uncovers the unconscious assumptions; it lays bare the collective soul of a generation far more frankly than any individual would reveal his own soul. The main messages of the twentieth-century arts are almost entirely opposed to the Christian message about man. Too often they preach disharmony, the meaninglessness of life, despair, degradation, hedonism and sadness where the Christian preaches serenity. This is not a complaint against twentieth-century art. Art is a reflection of life. The artist, the composer, the singer must be honest to their own generation. They serve all of us by telling us so clearly what is going on in the minds of our contemporaries.

Compare the artists of the seventeenth-century Dutch schools with the Italian artists before them and with Picasso after them. The Italians ignore the common man. They concentrate on an idealized man, Christ, the apostles and saints, and an idealized woman, the Madonna. The ordinary man is not worth painting. If he can acquire virtue from the saints he may perhaps – after years in purgatory – attain a place in heaven. But this depends on the saints and not on him. With the Reformation, the focus of attention – from Catholic artists as well as Protestant – switches to the common man; not only to the great merchants of Amsterdam, but to ordinary working men and women – Frans Hals' servants, for example, ordinary people whose life is significant, whose eyes are serene, whose characters are individual and who, above all, are given by the artist a certain natural dignity. Then we move on to Picasso. He still paints ordinary men and women, but all natural dignity has

49

gone. The faces are blank and hopeless and the symmetry and form has been deliberately distorted to make the whole effect accidental and meaningless. The image of man is degraded.[34]

Beautiful furnishings, fabrics and pottery are still being made, beautiful pictures are still being painted, crowds still flock to hear artists sing, play and perform great works of beauty. But they do not reflect the *Zeitgeist*. The spirit of the age has destroyed form and meaning and replaced them by disorder and cacophony. Meaning has been replaced by a blank – in one recent picture by a complete blank. (Even some architects feel the necessity to be either blank or brutal.) Tunes are being overtaken by noise and the beauties of nature have been replaced by deliberately meaningless pictures, the disconnected eye, the impression of a wild nightmare when nothing makes sense. Man is not only shown as a sensual machine but is deliberately degraded. Realism does not include dignity and beauty. It shows man as an animal that eats, drinks, excretes, copulates, fights and dies. It is this degraded view of man which the Christian must oppose with the dignity of man made in the image of God, responsible directly to God for all he does and says and taking his place as a responsible being in a divinely ordained social order.

Notes

1. See, for example, 1 Timothy 2:3f., 'God our Saviour, who desires all men to be saved,' and Matthew 28:19, 'Go therefore and make disciples of all nations.' *Cf.* also Luke 24:47; Acts 1:8.
2. Romans 12:2, 'Do not be conformed to this world but be transformed by the renewal of your mind.' The New Testament is full of examples, starting with the apostles; so also is the experience of the Christian church.
3. Matthew 10:30, 'Even the hairs of your head are all numbered.'
4. Paul says that he received mercy that Christ might display his perfect patience in him (1 Timothy 1:16). Throughout the Bible patience and long-suffering are attributed to God. *Cf.* Romans 15:5, AV: 'The God of patience.'
5. John 3:15.   6. Luke 23:43.   7. Hebrews 11:31.
8. Matthew 1:5.   9. John 4:1–42.
10. Matthew 9:11; Mark 2:16; Luke 15:2.   11. Luke 7:36.

12. Acts 9.   13. 1 Peter 2:12; 2:15; cf. Proverbs 16:7.

14. 1 Corinthians 5:9f.   15. Matthew 25:14–30; Luke 19:11–27.

16. See *The Social Problems of an Industrial Civilization* by Elton L. Mayo (Routledge & Kegan Paul, 1947), chapter 4, 'Hawthorne and the Western Electric Company'. Mayo writes: 'What actually happened was that six individuals became a team and the team gave itself wholeheartedly and spontaneously to cooperation in the experiment. The consequence was that they felt themselves to be participating freely and without afterthought, and were happy in the knowledge that they were working without coercion from above or limitation from below. They were themselves astonished at the consequence, for they felt that they were working less under pressure than ever before.'

17. Matthew 6:24; Luke 16:13.   18. John 8:36.

19. The Christian believes that man was created in the image of God; the animals were not. The humanist, while accepting the Christian view of the dignity of man, undermines it by classifying man as a higher class of animal, and the position from which he resists racialism is not nearly so strong.

20. James 2:1–7.

21. Galatians 3:28. See also Paul's greetings at the end of each Letter.

22. Proverbs 16:32, 'He who is slow to anger is better than the mighty, and he who rules his spirit than he who takes a city.'

23. We tolerate the rise in murder and violence when they are no more than statistics, but when a respected, wise and kindly colleague is murdered on his way home for the contents of his briefcase, violence no longer seems a tolerable side effect of the permissive society.

24. Genesis 9:5,6.

25. He constantly quoted from it, for instance in the account of the temptation in Matthew 4. He expounded it to the two disciples on the road to Emmaus. 'And beginning with Moses and all the prophets, he interpreted to them in all the scriptures the things concerning himself' (Luke 24:27). He refers often to Abraham. See, for example, John 8:58, 'Before Abraham was, I am.'

26. 2 Peter 2:5.   27. Romans 4:2ff.; Galatians 3:6ff.

28. Hebrews 7:1–19.

29. Romans 13:4. It is argued in the debate on capital punishment for capital offences against the state that hostages would be shot for every guerrilla who was executed. But hostages are already being taken and innocent people are already being shot in cold blood. The simple argument for capital punishment is that that particular murderer cannot murder again. But the stronger argument is that the attempt by the state to limit violence without capital punishment is experimental. If the view I put forward here is correct the attempt will fail and hundreds of innocent lives will be lost in the experiment. The failure by the state to protect its soldiers and police may also do lasting damage to the

confidence needed between government and those who are responsible for its physical security. If government is to command the absolute allegiance of the police and armed forces, it must not hazard their lives unnecessarily. These secular arguments are put forward, however, simply to show that what I believe to be the Christian principle is not unreasonable in the world as it is.

30. Romans 12:19.   31. Romans 13:1.   32. Genesis 2:18.
33. 1 Peter 1:6f.
34. This whole subject is dealt with extensively by H. R. Rookmaaker, in *Modern Art and the Death of a Culture* (Inter-Varsity Press, 1970). The author is Professor in the History of Art at the Free University, Amsterdam.

3 Family order

Marriage

The Christian teaching on marriage is that it was ordained by God for companionship between one man and one woman;[1] that it is a lifelong partnership built on love;[2] that the physical union creates 'one flesh',[3] and produces a mutual dependence;[4] that both partners must respect the wishes of the other,[5] but that the ultimate authority is with the husband;[6] that parents must care for their children;[7] and that children must obey their parents.[8]

Christian teaching also condemns every relationship and action which damages the family, including infidelity,[9] adultery,[10] fornication,[11] lust,[12] homosexuality[13] and incest.[14] It does not allow divorce, except for the innocent party in the case of adultery[15] – though some churches do not allow even this.

The first reason given for the existence of the family is, as we have seen above, that 'it is not good for man to be alone'. This is a profound truth. Today society is being atomized as children split from parents and parents split from each other, each spinning off into lonely orbits on their own. But we were not made to live alone. We need company, and the company of people who will not disappear when we most need them, people bound to us as we are bound to them, who will see us through a rough patch. Since we were not made to live alone, the stress of loneliness can be unbearable. A famous and popular actor was asked whether he had any conscience in walking out on his wife and family. He said that he had provided for them up to the hilt, and had given them everything they could possibly want. But, of course, he had not. They did not want money; they wanted him. A house, a car, a gardener and a chauffeur were no substitute for a father and husband.

Marriage is first of all about companionship. If marriage were primarily about the procreation of children it could be dissolved if the partners became incapable of having children. But marriage is first of all a binding alliance between close friends. A husband and wife should always have plenty to talk about, to argue about, to enthuse over. They need an interest in each other's activities inside and outside the home. They need to sharpen each other's wits, to laugh together. They need to rub off each other's cranky corners. And they need to carry each other through the rough patches – to convince the patient that they are not dying just yet, to restore an ego battered by the boss or the neighbour, to calm an indignation overflowing into self-righteous rage. And when the real tragedy does come, to suffer it together, each helping the other. That is what nine tenths of a marriage relationship is all about. If that part goes right, the physical side cannot go wrong for long. If that part goes wrong, the physical side is nothing better than licensed brutality.

Secondly, marriage is a lifelong partnership. When the Pharisees asked Jesus whether it was lawful to divorce one's wife for any cause, he said that husband and wife were no longer two but one. 'What therefore God has joined together, let no man put asunder.' He accepted that Moses had allowed divorce in the civil law, but went back to the moral law in the creation ordinance when he said, 'From the beginning it was not so.' His own position is firmly based on the moral law: 'And I say to you: whoever divorces his wife, except for unchastity, and marries another, commits adultery.'[16] This lifelong partnership, treating two as one, helps to give mutual trust.

Any lasting human relationship needs trust. Marriage needs complete trust. We lock the front door of the house for protection against those whom we do not trust. But there must be a place in our lives where we can relax, lower the guard, feel safe and secure. What we say and do within our own families and especially with our wives and husbands must be secure and privileged. We must not feel that we have to be on our guard in case there, too, someone is waiting to exploit our unguarded moment. Betrayal by friends is a shattering experience. The psalmist expresses it vividly.[17] But, in the nature of things, friendships cannot be for ever. We cannot depend on them completely. We have no right to insist that a friend does not move on. So friendship is never completely secure.

But if marriage is to be a relationship of complete trust, it must be completely secure. That means that all breaches in the relationship must be healed and that parting cannot be an option. Once a final breach is admitted as a possibility, the relationship is completely different. Neither partner can trust the other completely. Each has to think of the possibility of life apart, has to prepare a fall-back position. Dependence can go only so far; and ill health, mental stress, unemployment and old age are all sources of additional anxiety instead of being burdens to share. The Christian faith is not being harsh in insisting on a lifelong partnership. It is being realistic. We all need a lifelong partner. A living-in companion is not the same thing.

Marriage is also a physical union. Christ referred the Pharisees to the creation ordinance. Paul also quotes Genesis 2:24: 'For this reason a man shall leave his father and mother and be joined to his wife, and the two shall become one flesh.'[18] The physical union creates the commitment. That is the point at which the partners become 'one flesh', whether or not there has been a ceremony. A 'common-law wife' has the same moral rights as one who has been married in a church. The marriage depends on two people becoming 'one flesh', not on a particular form of vows. It is this union which creates the dependence. The woman, especially, becomes dependent on the man – 'her desire shall be for her husband'.[19] Once a physical union has been consummated, the breach of the union is almost always damaging to both parties, but especially to the woman. There is no such state as 'experimental marriage'. No-one can undo the dependence created by physical union; no-one can safeguard against the damage done by its breach. And a physical union which carries no firm commitment on either side imposes intolerable strains. If the strains are too much for it, that proves nothing about the potential compatibility of the partners in a true marriage.

This is not an argument for casual marriage. Christians believe in a religious marriage ceremony in order to underline the importance and permanence of marriage. This is not something which should be contracted hurriedly, thoughtlessly and without witnesses. It must be done before God and man. It should be witnessed by both families and by groups of friends, all those who must in future respect the relationship and help it. Casual association gives rise to all the same obligations, but it does not acknowledge them in public and this makes it easier to dismiss them in private. The major offence arises when the casual association is casually dissolved, when the man walks out on the woman or the woman walks out on the man.

Nor does this argument necessarily force people who have been promiscuous and then become Christians to take their last casual acquaintance through a Christian marriage ceremony. The whole way of life was wrong, and although Paul points out that Christians should not become 'one body' with a prostitute,[20] he does not suggest that those who have wrongly done so are to consider themselves bound to someone who is promiscuous for the rest of their lives. A promiscuous person is, in any case, almost certain to breach the bond by becoming 'one body' with someone else. But if the relationship is stable and genuine, then it should be confirmed and made permanent. A minister once had to advise a new convert who had left his wife over twenty years before and had a subsequent family by his mistress. Did he now have to find his legal wife and disown his mistress? The minister said No, and told him that his duty was to the people with whom he had been living for twenty years. There was no point in doubling his original misdeed by leaving those who needed him and going back to someone to whom he was now a stranger.

In a Christian marriage, both partners must respect the wishes of the other. Paul told the Corinthians, 'The husband should give to his wife her conjugal rights, and likewise the wife to her husband. For the wife does not rule over her own body, but the husband does; likewise the husband does not rule over his own body, but the wife does.'[21] Sex is not to be one-sided. It is right when both partners are willing and it is wrong if one partner is imposing on the other. Each must be generous with the other; each must fit in with the other's feelings. Neither is to withhold from the other – except by agreement, for prayer, and then only for a time.[22] Neither is to be over-demanding. That is the Christian rule in love and it is a rule which makes for greatest tenderness and the most lasting happiness.

Unstable relationships

The Christian is more saddened than shocked by promiscuity and divorce. Those who have a stable and happy marriage can only feel extremely sorry for those who do not. Unlike the man of the world, the Christian moves in both Christian and non-Christian circles and cannot help contrasting the happiness which comes from a secure marriage and mutual commitment with the terrible strain and stress which comes from insecure dependency. The idea that those who are insecure are somehow more free is ludicrous. Those who will not be bound by marriage have all the freedom of the acrobat on the high wire. One false move and they're clinging on for dear life.

The newspaper and magazine articles which try to advise you on how to keep your girl – or more often, your man – show the kind of strain which is put on the relationship. In all the articles and especially in the advertising there is, with today's emphasis on sex rather than companionship, a tendency to downgrade the wife to the status of a mistress. What the commercialized sex industry can never admit is that the greatest stimulant in marriage is the love which comes from mutual respect. Once this respect vanishes something goes out of the relationship which all the stimulants in the world can never replace. Indeed, the stimulants themselves seem progressively to deaden the natural instinct, so that the true relationship is never regained. Certainly the pastoral experience of churches, especially of city churches, is that the insecure and artificial relationships of today bring the most terrible personal problems and destroy the very faculty they set out to satisfy; whereas the security of

Christian marriage produces not only a stable family but also an incomparably richer personal relationship at every level.

Commercialized sex, on the other hand, takes no account of women or men as human beings. Sex, instead of being a part of the human relationship, becomes dominant. The fulfilment of sexual desires becomes the overriding urge and everything else is trampled out of the way. The woman is not a human being with a personality and spirit, but a 'doll' with particular physical statistics to be used and left, an object of lust and not of love. Commercialized sex leads to the exploitation of the weak by the strong, of the inexperienced by the experienced. It is corrupting because it becomes progressively more difficult for someone who becomes used to sex as an expression of lust to treat it as the supreme expression of one person's respect and love for another. In popular fiction the man who sows his wild oats turns with the greatest of ease to a deep and lasting love. In real life it is not so easy. As one girl says to the other in the *New Yorker* cartoon, 'He's one of those "Life-began-the-day-I-met-you" type of men.'

Functional authority within the family

Christian marriage does not make the woman subservient to the man. In the traditional marriage service the wife vows to obey her husband. But Paul is more explicit. He says that the husband is the head of the wife as Christ is the head of the church.[23] As Christ loved the church and gave his life for it, so the husband must love his wife and be prepared to sacrifice everything for her. Christian obedience springs from love and it must be the same in the family. It is the husband who has the greater responsibility and the husband who must make the greater sacrifice. In practice the business of making the final decision is functional. The wife gives her husband the benefit of her unstinted advice and he makes the decision and takes the responsibility. In many of the families I know the husband seems to find it much easier to accept responsibility than the wife. Most of the wives seem inclined to worry about responsibility, to want to change their minds and to wonder whether they took the wrong decision. But the husbands will generally make up their minds and get on with it. Our own friends may not be a scientific example, but they are probably a fairly typical cross-section. And in families where the wife is dominant, where there is no final court of appeal as issues are bandied back between husband and wife, the result seems to be endless bickering not only between parents, but between children and between children and parents.

So the Christian social order gives the final authority to the husband, but it is a functional authority only. His decisions must be based on his responsibility to care for his wife and children. He must put their needs before his own. He must command the respect of his family because he loves them. As a Christian he cannot demand the satisfaction of his own wilfulness or indulgence.

It is often difficult for us to realize the difference between functional authority and dominance. The Romans called it *primus inter pares* – first among equals. The aim of a happy marriage is to have such a close sympathy and understanding that the question of final authority hardly ever arises, and in the rare cases where it does the decision is made with care and kindness and accepted in the same spirit.

That does not mean that the authority given to the head of the family can exist only if the rest of the family are perfect. The more imperfect the family, the more there is a need for someone to have the last word. If some final functional authority is needed even in the Trinity, how much more is it needed in an imperfect and bickering group of human beings. But the dominant father of the Victorian novels who used his own authority for his own ends is no more entitled to claim Christian authority than the rebellious son. One is abusing authority, the other is flouting it. Both are wrong.

Parents and children

Christian teaching lays down the duties within the family, not only of parents to each other but also of parents to children and of children to each other and to their parents. It also includes mutual duties within the wider patriarchal family of grandparents, uncles, aunts and cousins.[24] There must be no breaches in this circle of love and respect and all owe a duty to help each other. Parents are told, for instance, to save for their children,[25] fathers are told not to provoke their children to anger,[26] and many of Christ's parables about God the Father draw on the analogy of a human parent and his children.

Every child needs a father and a mother, separately and together. Every child needs the combination of discipline and love which is unique to the family. Our children must know that we love them not just because we feed, clothe and nurse them when they are sick, but because we listen to them, answer their questions, teach them games, take them to football matches and on holiday, sympathize when they are hurt, banter with them, enjoy their company and encourage them in their hobbies, help them with their homework and show them in a hundred different ways that they matter. So when we say, 'Don't do that', they know that we say it because we care for them, and however much they argue, they respect us. Even if they do not see the sense of what we say, they obey us because they love us and do not want to hurt us.

No parent is perfect and that is why two parents are so much better than one. Mum can calm Dad down when he overdoes it – and vice versa. The combination of two parents is likely to be reasonable more often than one alone. One parent can sort out the other's obsessions. And when there is a junior revolution, it is necessary for both parents to stand side by side – or back to back! Though many a widow works wonders, the strain of bringing up a lively bunch of youngsters is best shared. No man has the right to walk out and leave it to his wife and no woman has the right to walk out and leave it to her husband.

And each parent has a separate contribution. A father cannot provide a mother's feminine influence for his sons. He cannot help his daughter as a woman can. On the other hand a father has something to contribute to his daughter which she does not get from her mother. But a father can help his sons to become men in a way a woman cannot.

The extended family

Within a wider family circle which has less intimacy, but wider variety of personality and experience, and where the permanence of the relationship still creates an atmosphere of security and trust, aunts, uncles and cousins all help with encouragement and advice. A young aunt will listen when mum is too busy. An uncle will explain how to sail a boat or fix a stereo when father doesn't understand how to mend a fuse. And cousins you have known for years will talk far into the night about problems you wouldn't trust to temporary friends at school.

In times of trouble the extended family can also rally round. The terrible loneliness of a widow can be softened by brothers, sisters, sons, daughters and grandchildren. Financial disasters can be averted and financial success shared. Many a person has been helped on the way by an uncle with some money to spare. Paul told Timothy that nephews should help their widowed aunts so that their needs did not fall on the slender funds of the church.[27] And long-term burdens – handicapped children, for example, or dotty uncles – can be borne if they are shared. No member of the patriarchal family is ever alone, no burden is borne alone. And on the happier occasions – births, weddings, graduations, promotions – all the family are there to give support and encouragement.

The extended family is a music-hall joke. But all jokes are based on life. There is a real relationship which exists. In an imperfect world it is an imperfect relationship. But the sponging cousins, the alcoholic uncle, the shockable aunt, the formidable mother-in-law, your wife's brother's little horrors, would not matter if they did not have some claim to cross your threshold. It is the recognition of this claim which creates the situations which Giles illustrates so wonderfully in the London *Daily Express*. If grandmas did not exist, Giles would never have been able to draw their caricature. But formidable though grandma may be, she still has a secure place at the fireside of her long-suffering son-in-law.

The intellectuals of our generation have put the extended family in the balance against personal freedom and have decided that personal freedom is the greater good. The old romantic story tells of the heroine choosing the man she loves instead of the man approved by her family. Being a romance, it does not say where she turns when they have their first row, whose advice she asks when she cannot get the baby to sleep at night and what happens when he finally walks out. The new realism does not give a constructive answer but it does at least recognize the problems. But the Christian social order is a matter of balance. If marriage is to be a lifelong companionship it must have love. The cold, calculating family alliance, devoid of all feeling and romance, is wrong. So is the refusal to take any notice of the views of parents, brothers and sisters.

The precious and irreplaceable web of relationships is broken when the marriage is broken. The bubbling gaiety, the irrepressible humour of the secure family circle is gone for ever. Children become pawns in an adults' quarrel and, in their turn, play one parent off against the other. The quarrel or the satisfaction of a parent's lust matters more than they do. Is it much wonder they become embittered, and that all too often the chip on their shoulder makes them a menace to society?

Broken marriages

Today we tend to underrate the extent of the damage caused by the disruption of the family. The church, with its duty to care for the distressed, is constantly faced with this terrible problem of children who cannot sleep at night worrying about their parents, with suicides and threatened suicides, with unwanted babies who cannot smile and with the widespread problem of juvenile delinquency which is almost always associated with a broken home. Sometimes the wider family can pick up the pieces and children are taken in by aunts, uncles and grandparents. But what is going to happen when the grandparents no longer live together? Today's generation is relying on the stability of its elders. But what stability is it giving to its own children when they marry and have problems? A stable family will tend to produce a stable family, but an unstable family is setting its own example to those who follow on.

Even families which try to keep to Christian standards will quarrel and be tempted to infidelity. But those with Christian standards will do their best to put things right, will attempt to swallow pride, will be held by their obligations, will not be tempted by the specious argument that the children would be better off with parents who get on together. But if parents can part from each other, then a stepmother or stepfather can disappear too. The family, from being a secure base, becomes just another temporary and uncertain relationship. Once admit that the family can split, then security has gone for good. This gives an irresponsible parent, and especially a father, the most terrible sanction. Natural feelings are stronger in a mother than in a father. It is easier for fathers to get a job than it is for a mother. So it is easier for a father to walk out. If fathers who walk out can insist on divorce, then the family is helpless. Since the threat to walk out is unequal, the right to divorce at will gives the father the power to insist that the family plays to his tune. It undermines the dignity and rights of women and children.

The state tries to meet the needs of women and children by giving them rights outside the family. The state pays a family allowance to wives; it is beginning to insist on equal pay for women. It is even suggested that women have a legal right to be paid housekeeping money. But no legal rights are any substitute for a social order which insists that women be treated as partners.

The generation gap

Society is said to be suffering today from rebellious youth. There is a sense, of course, in which youth is always rebellious, always questioning the hypocrisies of its elders, always refusing to accept the conventional wisdom. But today's rebellion goes much much further. The combination of universal state-aided education, well-paid jobs and the welfare state has made children financially independent of their parents for the first time in history. Fathers have no financial sanction. Indeed, because 'the rate for the job' in industry is the same for all adults of whatever age, the son with no responsibilities may earn as much as his father who still has to house,

63

feed and clothe his mother and the younger members of the family. And because incomes in different types of work are paid by supply and demand as much as by merit, the son may earn more than his father even though he may not have his father's skill. In addition, there is the widening of education which gives the next generation more learning without necessarily giving them more wisdom. There is also a real difference in outlook. The fathers had morality without faith. The children naturally ask why. All these are the patent cause of a generation gap which is far deeper and wider than the normal differences between one generation and the next.

The result is a generation which is less governed by the discipline of family life than any before it. The 'discretionary' income of the young – the income over and above their basic needs – is several times the 'discretionary' income of the family man; and they are the big spenders. Whole industries are based on their expenditure. This high income enables them to live away from home if they wish. And even if they do live at home, they can create their own life-style, spend their spare time in their own cars, go to their own entertainment spots. Given a stable home background, none of this might matter very much. But the rising rate of divorce, almost certainly reflecting a much higher number of unhappy homes, is cutting off a rising proportion of the young from any home life at all. Every violent youngster had a mother and a father. When parents turn the children out of the home to fend for themselves, when the home is a scene of constant violence and abuse, when the child receives no encouragement, no love, no kindness, no sympathy, no helping hand, it is small wonder that their frustrated loyalty goes to the gang. And if they are not encouraged to play a part in adult society it is not surprising if they form their own society, make their own rules, exact their own tribute, impose their own discipline and police their own patch with their own weapons.

And wherever in the social scale money is the god, wherever worldly wealth dominates the conversation, it is little wonder that there is a reaction against materialism. It is understandable that even a wave of middle-class children should opt out or join anti-capitalist or materialist movements. And it is understandable that they should argue that there is little difference between the alcohol of the parents and their own soft drugs. The sins of the parents are visited on the children to the third and fourth generation. But two wrongs do not make a right. One extreme can be as wrong as the other. A parent may not be able to say 'Do as I do', but there may still be wisdom in his objective 'Do as I tell you'.

Christians generally believe that the lack of parental authority, the inability of the older generation to hand on accumulated wisdom to its sons and daughters and to protect them from their inexperience, causes major damage to society. As Paul pointed out, the command to honour father and mother was the first command which had a promise attached to it. The promise was that the society which kept the command would benefit directly – 'that it may be well with you and that you may live long . . .'.[28] Paul makes the same point in his Letter to the Colossians,[29] and in the Old Testament the same theme is found, especially in the book of Proverbs.[30] It is fair to read into all this a warning that the generation which throws over the accumulated wisdom of parents and grandparents is likely to suffer.

Despite the bright clothes, the much-vaunted liberation and the money, the pop generation seems plaintive and sad and the philosophy seems introspective, existential and despairing. It certainly seems to lack the cheerful note of challenge and achievement. It has the sickly colour of a fungus which lives off the energy of the healthy stock.

This is just a trend, of course, and not a universal truth. Many of the present generation are less hypocritical, far gentler, more thoughtful and far more devoted to good causes than were their hearty, thoughtless, beer-drinking, back-slapping fathers, who accepted atomic warfare without a qualm. But the trend is strong and it matters because it shows the beginning of a volatile and unstable society, a society which has lost its roots.

Those who preach the cult of youth, who have renounced the wisdom of the ages, may argue that roots do not matter, that the old plant is rotten, that society is perhaps all the better for being replanted with fresh stock and fresh ideas. But that is not the

Christian view. Youth is a false god. The Christian does not believe in some inevitable evolutionary process which makes each generation wiser than the last. Wisdom comes from experience and experience has to be transmitted. The wisdom of Solomon is as relevant today as it was when the book of Proverbs was written. It is a wise son who listens to his father, a foolish one who ignores all that has gone before. It is a wise father who exercises authority, a foolish father who forgets the ignorance of the young.

The attack on the family

The family is now under attack from all sides. Each attack is justified as a contribution to personal liberty, but together they do immense damage to the institution of the family and all of us suffer more loss from this attack than we can ever recover from the supposed liberty we gain in exchange. Divorce, sex outside the marriage bond and homosexual relationships are condemned by Christ and the apostles and by the law and the prophets before them. We may argue whether homosexual practices should be dealt with by civil law, and about the grounds for civil divorce, but there can be no argument on the moral case. The fact that some people are peculiarly susceptible to temptation to homosexual acts by their genetic make-up does not make them morally right. Others are peculiarly tempted by their genetic make-up to violence, the very poor are peculiarly tempted to theft, the very rich to avarice. All of us are subject to temptation and we must have the same compassion as Christ for sinners. But we must condemn the sin as he did, seeing homosexual practices as offences against the divine order which are patently and particularly perverse. The revulsion which most people feel against the practice is only natural and not to be regarded as mere lack of tolerance. The Christian must help and try to understand those who are susceptible and fight against it; but he must also be free to challenge those who put it forward as a perfectly acceptable and natural way of life.

Lust is also condemned and excavations of ancient cities show that pornography is as old as civilization. But the commercial exploitation of lust through the pornographic industry is new. The cameras and the modern systems of mass production and distribution make an impact of an order completely different from anything that has gone before and needs special mention.

Christians are troubled not so much by pornography as by the attitudes of people to each other which create the demand for pornography and the effect of these attitudes on the happiness and stability of society. The Christian is worried, in particular, that pornography, violence and the widespread use of drugs are all the result of the same dehumanizing trend.

The Christian's first question is whether pornography is compatible with a Christian view of the dignity of men and women. Is a pornographic picture of a woman – or man – with its aim of arousing sexual passion, likely to produce a feeling of respect for the human dignity of the person in the picture, or is it likely to degrade them? Very few people would want to see their wives, mothers, sisters or daughters in a pornographic picture because of the innate feeling that this kind of picture detracts from human dignity. Pornography has a strong dehumanizing trend. It may be that the pornography *voyeur* can disassociate the picture he sees from the women he meets, but one is entitled to doubt it. The trend in dress – or rather undress – in advertising seems to have followed the tendency to make women into sexual objects rather than rational human beings. The dehumanizing trend in literature goes in the same direction and women seem to be treated increasingly as objects of sexual gratification rather than as people to be loved.

The Christian view of pornography can be stated very briefly. One of the Ten Commandments is 'You shall not commit adultery', and Christ interpreted this very strictly. He said, 'Every one who looks at a woman lustfully has already committed adultery with her in his heart.'[31]

Christian teaching confirmed by pastoral experience tells us that lust is a cancer which destroys the personality of the individual. His relationships with others, not only with those who are closest to him, but also their friends in a wider circle, are progressively spoiled.

'Desire when it has conceived gives birth to sin; and sin when it is full-grown brings forth death.'[32] Whether the lust is for sex or for anything else, it is essentially selfish and anti-social. The apostle Peter says, 'Abstain from the passions of the flesh that wage war against your soul.'[33] There is hardly any sexual perversion practised today which is not condemned in the Bible, and there is certainly no sexual perversion recorded in the Bible which is not practised today. But the message is consistently the same in the Bible then and in the church now, that perversions cannot be treated lightly. They are an acquired taste, but once acquired they grow and then they dominate and then they destroy.

The pornographic trade reflects a progression from titillation to mild pornography, then to hard pornography, then to super-hard pornography, and then there is always something beyond even that. In parallel with the progression in pornography is an increasing discussion of the problem of impotence. The unnatural stimulation seems to destroy the natural until finally there is no reaction except to the most extreme stimulation. Of course this does not happen in a month or even a year. But if it is happening at all, the individual is put under bondage to a force outside himself which he is less and less capable of controlling. And if it is happening at all it is bound to have some effect, however small, on the natural place of sex in marriage. No marriage is perfect, but the Christian view is that marriage can be improved only if the partners help each other. If one of the partners is subjecting himself or herself to strong stimulation outside marriage, then the partnership and harmony within marriage is damaged and this is a fraud on the other partner. And if someone who is not married is accustomed to pornographic stimulation, then, when he does marry, he may not be able to offer equal partnership.

In other words, both have a right to expect that the other partner will bring to this most intimate part of the marriage partnership the whole of this side of their life. That is the Christian ideal. In the experience of the Christian church, marriages in which Christian standards are observed are, all else being equal, far happier than those in which they are not. The families are more stable and the problems far fewer. Indeed, marriage where both partners submit to Christian standards gives a measure of happiness in an uncertain world which makes those who enjoy it feel that, of all human satisfaction, this is the greatest, and that anything which prevents people from finding this supreme enjoyment rates fairly low in the scale of human priorities.

The strongest protectors of the pornographic industry are those who fear that any curb on it would endanger the principle of free speech. But in defending free speech one has to defend a defensible line. And in most countries today it would be easier to defend freedom of speech if one did not have to include pornography. One can well imagine some cultural commissar making the point that freedom of speech is all very well but, as can be seen from the capitalist countries, it opens the way to a flood of pornography and the exploitation of the people by unscrupulous commercial interests. It is true that pornography, like blasphemy, expresses a point of view. But so does racialism and so do libels and slanders, all of which are placed outside the protection of free speech because they tend to bring particular people or groups of people into disrepute, hatred or contempt.

Most of today's advocates of free speech are liberals living in a liberal society, where the danger to free speech is limited and the personal danger to them in advocating free speech is also limited. One's guess is that those who have to suffer for freedom – intellectuals, writers, poets and religious minorities in countries where communication of ideas is censored – would sooner not be lumbered with a defence of pornography.

Although in a limited sense pornography can be said to be the expression of an idea, in the vast majority of cases it is simply the sale of a commodity – a sexual stimulant. If pornography is the sale of a commodity then the commodity should be judged as other commodities are judged, and in the church's judgment the claims made for it are fraudulent and the public should be warned against it. The commodity purports to satisfy the sexual instinct, but it is, in the general experience of Christian pastors, an addictive commodity which by overstimulation destroys the instinct and degrades the person. To associate it with freedom of speech is to downgrade the whole argument for human liberty.

Notes

1. Monogamy was the divine order in the beginning. Adam had one wife and this seems to have been the early rule. The Old Testament tells of men of faith who took second wives, but in every case it also tells of the trouble this brought them. The church reinstated the original rule as an absolute necessity for elders (see 1 Timothy 3:2; Titus 1:6) and an example for all Christians. As the status of women became established, it became the rule for all Christians.
2. Ephesians 5:25, 'Husbands, love your wives, as Christ loved the church and gave himself up for her.'
3. Ephesians 5:31, 'For this reason a man shall leave his father and mother and be joined to his wife, and the two shall become one flesh.' It is difficult to see room for polygamy in this model of marriage. Monogamy is clearly the divine order set out here.
4. Genesis 3:16, 'To the woman he said . . . your desire shall be for your husband.' The mutual duties set out in Ephesians 5 also imply a mutual dependence.
5. Ephesians 5:21, 'Be subject to one another.'
6. Ephesians 5:23, 'The husband is the head of the wife as Christ is the head of the church.'
7. 2 Corinthians 12:14, 'Children ought not to lay up for their parents, but parents for their children'; Ephesians 6:4, 'Fathers, do not provoke your children to anger.' Many of Christ's parables, including the parable of the prodigal son, illustrate the ideal of the father's love for his children.
8. Ephesians 6:1, 'Children, obey your parents in the Lord, for this is right.'
9. Malachi 2:14ff., 'The Lord was witness to the covenant between you and the wife of your youth, to whom you have been faithless, though she is your companion and your wife by covenant . . . So take heed to yourselves and do not be faithless.'
10. Exodus 20: 14, 'You shall not commit adultery.' See also Deuteronomy 5:18; Matthew 5:27; 19:18; Romans 13:9.
11. 1 Corinthians 6:12–20, 'The body is not meant for immorality, but for the Lord' (verse 13). 'Shun immorality. Every other sin which a man commits is outside the body; but the immoral man sins against his own body' (verse 18). See also Galatians 5:19; Ephesians 5:3; Colossians 3:5; 1 Thessalonians 4:3.
12. Matthew 5:28, 'Every one who looks at a woman lustfully has already committed adultery with her in his heart.'

13. Leviticus 18:22.   14. Leviticus 18:6.

15. Matthew 19:9, 'Whoever divorces his wife, except for unchastity, and marries another, commits adultery: and he who marries a divorced woman commits adultery' (RSV margin). It is on the basis of this exception that many Christian churches allow the remarriage of the innocent party. But it is clear from Christ's words that this is the only exception.

16. See Matthew 19:3–9.   17. See Psalms 41:9; 55:12–14.

18. Ephesians 5:31.   19. Genesis 3:16.   20. 1 Corinthians 6:15f.

21. 1 Corinthians 7:3f.   22. 1 Corinthians 7:5.

23. Ephesians 5:23.

24. The laws of consanguinity assumed that this wider family was an intimate group. See above, p. 32, note 45, on Leviticus 18:6–18. The detailed relationships are spelt out in stories throughout the Bible (see, *e.g.*, the story in Acts 23:16–24 of the apostle Paul's nephew who saved his uncle from ambush by his alertness) and in specific commands.

25. See note 7 above.   26. See note 7 above.

27. 1 Timothy 5:4, AV.   28. Ephesians 6:1–3.

29. Colossians 3:20.   30. *E.g.*, Proverbs 13:1.

31. Matthew 5:28.   32. James 1:15.   33. 1 Peter 2:11.

4 Civil order

Governments are instituted by God

Christ and the two great apostles all teach quite clearly and explicitly that civil governments are divinely ordained institutions and that it is the duty of the Christian to obey them. Christ, when asked about the duty of Jews to pay taxes to the Roman Empire, said, 'Render to Caesar the things that are Caesar's.'[1] Their coinage, Christ pointed out, bore Caesar's head. He was the recognized ruler. He had his function and required his legal dues. On another occasion, when the disciples tried to defend Jesus against arrest, he told them not to resist, 'for all who take the sword will perish by the sword'.[2]

Peter said, 'Be subject for the Lord's sake to every human institution, whether it be to the emperor as supreme, or to governors as sent by him to punish those who do wrong and to praise those who do right.'[3] But the longest and most explicit statement comes from Paul.

Let every person be subject to the governing authorities. For there is no authority except from God, and those that exist have been instituted by God. Therefore he who resists the authorities resists what God has appointed, and those who resist will incur judgment. For rulers are not a terror to good conduct, but to bad. Would you have no fear of him who is in authority? Then do what is good, and you will receive his approval, for he is God's servant for your good. But if you do wrong, be afraid, for he does not bear the sword in vain; he is the servant of God to execute his wrath on the wrongdoer. Therefore one must be subject, not only to avoid God's wrath but also for the sake of conscience. For the same reason you also pay taxes, for the authorities are ministers of God, attending to this very thing. Pay all of them their dues, taxes to whom taxes are due, revenue to whom revenue is due, respect to whom respect is due, honour to whom honour is due.[4]

The only exception to this rule is if civil government commands us to disobey God. We obey civil government because it is ordained of God and God commands obedience. If civil government tells us to disobey God, it destroys its own authority. We are to 'render to Caesar the things that are Caesar's, *and* to God the things that are God's'. The Jewish rulers called the apostles before them 'and charged them not to speak or teach at all in the name of Jesus. But Peter and John answered them, "Whether it is right in the sight of God to listen to you rather than to God, you must judge; for we cannot but speak of what we have seen and heard." '[5]

These are commands which many have found hard to obey; but down the centuries they have been followed because doctrines taught by Christ and the two great apostles, Paul and Peter, must in the end be accepted by those professing to be Christians.

It must have been especially difficult for the early Christians to accept that the secular power of their time, the Roman Empire, was ordained of God. Many of them were Jews and to them Romans were alien conquerors who had no right in their holy city. The Roman governor had condemned Christ to death on trumped-up charges which he did not believe.[6] They, themselves, had been imprisoned and persecuted for their faith and for their refusal to worship the emperor. Paul and Peter had been imprisoned, and James had been killed by Herod.[7]

The Roman government was imperialist. It did not have the legitimacy which we now attribute to nationalist governments, which, even if arbitrary, do at least represent their own people. The Roman government was certainly not representative. The democratic institutions of Rome had been thrown over by the Caesars and the carefully balanced constitution abandoned. And it was a corrupt government; as we learn from Paul's own imprisonment, governors expected to receive bribes.[8] Under political pressure Pilate allowed an admittedly innocent man to die. So our obedience to the laws is not to depend on our personal assessment of the government's worth. It is enough that it is the legitimate government.[9]

The restraint of government is more exact and therefore more limited than moral restraint. The church tells people what they ought to do in general terms; the state says what they must do in precise terms. The church deals with the internal man of conscience; the state can deal only with the external acts. The difference shows in the contrast between the moral law, embodied in the Ten Commandments, and the Jewish civil law, the Mosaic code. Christ points out that the limited legal obligation is not enough. The Mosaic code had to allow divorce for the hardness of their hearts, 'but from the beginning it was not so'.[10]

Government, when framing legislation, must take into account the hardness of men's hearts; it must not try to impose laws which society will not allow to be enforced. If it does, it will simply bring the law into disrepute. But there must be a civil power. As Paul explains in the passage quoted above, the 'powers that be' are needed to restrain evil and encourage good and they are entitled to bear the sword to maintain civil order. Conscience is not enough. There is evil in man which must be physically restrained as well as the good which must be encouraged.

Mankind, in fact, has never been able to get on without some form of civil government. Whenever it disappears there is anarchy; and all the evil, which in better times is restrained, comes pouring out unchecked. Between retreating and advancing armies, in unpoliced areas in civil wars, terrible crimes are committed on a horrifying scale. The weak, innocent and helpless are completely at the mercy of the strong and heartless. Those who want to help are too terrified to move. A youth with a gun or a knife can destroy the kindest and wisest in a moment of arrogant self-assertion. The *Pax Romana* of the tyrannical Roman Empire was a reality. Centuries after the great Empire had lost all real power, its name and reputation lived on in men's minds and they remembered not the tyranny, but the protection it had given against warring tribes. In Britain it lived on in the Arthurian legend of the great king and his knights who protected the innocent from the terror of marauding tribes in the dark ages after the Roman rule had ended.

But in more peaceful times, when men are not faced with the straight alternatives of strong rule or chaos, they demand that their civil law must have a moral base. Christians must agree with this and in a free society must argue for a Christian moral base. In a society which is not free, such as the Roman Empire, they must set a standard of morality in the community of Christians which, by its evident rightness and power of example, makes its impact on an alien society. The Christian faith is now well known. It has for centuries, by precept and practice, tamed principalities and powers and made rulers realize that there is a limit to their powers, that they, too, are accountable to a higher authority. It is widely known and respected, even where it is not practised. If people now want another moral base to the law, then they should set out their own full moral rules for critical examination. They should say what evidence they have that their order will be better, that its side effects will be manageable. They should show that they have real evidence of human behaviour under such changed conditions and that they are not proposing an experiment without any certainty of the outcome. Picking holes here and there in Christian morality is not the same thing as producing an acceptable alternative morality. And mere assertions that this or that part of Christian morality cannot be proved necessary are not enough.

Christian morality advocates the protection of the weak against the strong. It says that society should protect those who cannot protect themselves, for example children, the old, the weak, the disabled, the sick, the poor and, when they need such protection, women. And it has to protect property in so far as this is necessary to protect people. The Jewish civil code, set out in Exodus, Leviticus and Numbers, illustrates an interpretation of a moral code by a civil power. The Jewish civil code aims to protect the average man and to restore to him anything which has been expropriated by the rich and powerful.

Naturally, those who can protect themselves tend to resent interference by government. They include the rich and powerful – those with accumulated fortunes who want to keep them, those with high incomes who do not want to be taxed, and those workers with strong bargaining power who know that fair wage policies will restrain them from taking a rising share of incomes from their less powerful fellow workers. This is understandable. What is odd is the occasional alliance with these powerful groups by idealists who want to overthrow the 'system', under the mistaken impression that freedom from the shackles of the state will produce an ideal egalitarian society. Their error is to underestimate the evil in human nature, to attribute it entirely to the repression of the state and to believe, therefore, that the removal of the state will lead to the removal of evil. Those who feel like this should ask themselves who, if the power of the state disappears, is going to collect the wealth from the rich to pay for the social security of the poor.

The welfare state at risk in Great Britain and other democracies

The present welfare state in Britain and elsewhere goes as far as any state has ever done to protect the weaker members of society. It has instituted universal education, universal health services and universal social security. It has financed these by high and progressive taxation, bearing most heavily on higher incomes. It has undertaken to maintain high employment, to provide decent housing and steadily rising real incomes. All of this is in accordance with the Christian principle of caring for the weak and needy. No government would willingly reverse these policies; yet they are almost all at risk because they no longer have the full support of the moral order.

Universal education is at risk because of the breakdown of the family. Where the family is secure and parents care about children, the children benefit from free education. But where the authority of the family has collapsed, where there are no parents to support the teacher, teachers are quite incapable of educating those older children who no longer wish to be educated. Schools deteriorate into a blackboard jungle where the teacher is no longer in control.

And as society gives greater priority to material needs than to education, teachers fall behind in pay as well as in working conditions. It is a far cry from the days of Cromwell when teachers were thought so important that they were exempt from taxation!

The universal health service is at risk because the pay of doctors and nurses has lagged behind that of other workers.

The protection of young and old may also be undermined by the pressure for abortion and euthanasia. A minority of abortions must be necessary to protect the mother, but who can believe that as many as 30% of pregnancies have to be aborted in order to do this? And who can believe that this diversion of effort is not damaging to those who are really ill and in need of care? If euthanasia is legalized, how long will it be possible to maintain the ideal of a health service as a protection of life? Once a doctor administers death as well as life, his relationship with the patient changes. Who is to decide to take away life? Is the patient capable of deciding? Is the relative disinterested? Should the doctor have the power? The Christian view is that only God, who gave life, can take it away and that, with the exception of the state in judicial process and in protection of society, no-one else should ever have the power.

Social security, the payment of money to those who are ill, impoverished and out of work, has been called in question by its abuse. The apostle Paul's blunt principle was, 'If anyone will not work, let him not eat.'[11] If he *cannot* work, that is not his fault. But social security now protects those who *will* not work, and every authority knows that their number is now uncomfortably high. It is now possible to finance strikers by using social security for the wives and children of those on strike, instead of union funds. This brings the ideals of social security into disrepute and gives unnecessary ammunition to those who feel that a working man should fend for himself.

The continual attacks on the power of government undermines the discipline on which that government relies for the collection of taxes on higher incomes.

Policies of full employment come under pressure when the resulting scarcity of key workers is exploited to produce wage and salary increases which are far beyond any possible improvement in their productivity. Most ministers strenuously resist deflationary policies and try to maintain full employment. They recognize the need for restraint in trades-union bargaining if the dead end of continuously high unemployment is to be avoided. But there is very strong pressure on national treasuries to combat inflation by allowing unemployment to rise, and if the national currency is weak because of inflation they do not always have much choice.

Government provision for the needs of the citizen

The provision of decent housing in a healthy environment is an object which Christians, believing in the dignity of man, will support. But decent and healthy housing depends overwhelmingly on the regulation of development by governmental physical planning. The shanty-town slums show us what can happen if government does not have the power to do this. But while everyone wants better housing in general, no-one wants it next door to his own particular house. Every planning application brings instant opposition from the neighbours. If we are to avoid shanty towns and slums we must be prepared to give government reasonable power for physical planning.

The relief of poverty in both developed and developing nations would seem a proper objective of Christian morality. There can be little wrong and much that is right in trying to feed, clothe and house the human population better than they have been fed, clothed and housed before. Such policies depend on individual morality, on efforts to contribute much more to the economy than we take out. But individual efforts need to be supported, not frustrated, by government, and some mechanism has to mesh the efforts of individuals with each other and with government.

Most advanced societies find the need for economic planning. The time-span of industrial decision-making has lengthened considerably, and about half of industry needs about three years to turn expansion decisions into physical investment. These decisions can get badly out of phase and result, for example, in the expansion of

the motor industry beyond the country's road building or oil refining capacity, expansion of orders for the construction industry
beyond the available supply of workers, expansion of industry as a
whole beyond the country's capacity to finance it. All parts of the
high-income industrial economy are heavily interdependent. A
sudden stop in the flow of components or raw materials, or a sudden
drying up of markets, can be disastrous. So decisions in major industries have to be related to each other through some kind of
national planning process.

It should be remembered that all economic setbacks fall especially
hard on those who are weakest. Policies of national planning are
clearly put at risk by economic Darwinism which positively rejoices
in the survival of the fittest at the expense of the weakest, and which
preaches that the weak should go to the wall and is perfectly prepared to see firms crash and thousands of people pour on to a labour
market which cannot possibly absorb them.

Paul tells the Colossians that their work force is to be treated
justly and fairly.[12] Most governments in advanced economies now
try to have fair-wage guidelines and laws on minimum wages. But
economic Darwinism attacks fair-wage policies on the grounds that
wages should be fixed only by supply and demand, that the powerful
are entitled to more and the weak must expect less. If the open
market results in an inflationary spiral, then demand must be reduced and unemployment increased until an economic equilibrium
is reached. This economic determinism does not believe that free
men are capable of taking any view except one of self-interest. Shop-
floor power which jacks up wages by holding production lines to
ransom is directly opposed to the duty of government to look after
those who have no power to jack up their incomes. The continued
use of shop-floor power to extract a higher share of national income
is a direct cause of inflation, and the resultant depreciation of the
currency has the effect of transferring money forcibly from the weak
to the powerful. Ever since the first king put his head on the first
coin, governments have been responsible for preserving the value
of the currency so that all who accept it receive back full value
whenever they want.

The Christian believes in the dignity of the individual and in protecting him from violence. But the basic duty of government to give physical protection is now called in question. The police and the courts are often held in contempt by those who oppose the power of the state. But it is the prime duty of law and the courts to protect the citizen against attack. If the police do not receive support, then protection is either not available or available only at a price that the rich can pay. As the police receive less support and as their relative income falls, so the private security agencies flourish, the incorruptibility of the police is no longer taken for granted, and universal protection against crime is almost impossible to maintain.

Different political systems

Although both state and church are ordained by God, there is an almost complete absence of dogma on the method of appointing the governments of either institution. Christian teaching is quite clear on the ends; it leaves the means open. We are told what elders and deacons should be like, but not precisely how they should be appointed.[13] So if a particular method of appointment does not produce the right kind of elder, it may be exchanged for one which does. No-one can justify and defend ineffective elders because they were appointed by a particular method. Similarly, there is no particular method of government which is sacrosanct. Different moral orders in society may require different types of government. Different nations may respond in different ways. Hard times may need one kind of government, easy times another. Education may make an immense difference to the type of government.

But since most countries with a predominantly Protestant ethic have developed as democracies, there must be a strong link between post-Reformation Christian principles and democratic government. Most Christians probably feel that they have a strong stake in the preservation of democratic institutions. A reversion to autocratic government would be a severe setback to the Christian social order which is based on the dignity and responsibility of the individual.

But as the Protestant ethic seems to have encouraged democratic institutions, its disappearance would almost certainly undermine them.

Democracy is based on a respect for the view of the individual citizen, an understanding that disputes are conducted by reason and not by force, and an agreement between opponents that the view of the majority will prevail. The Christian believes that all are answerable individually to God; that all have a conscience and are made in the image of God; that the state is there to serve the individual, and not the other way round. So the form of government in which the individual citizen is most important is nearest to the Christian ideal.

It is also a Christian principle that differences should be settled by reason. God is a God of reason and man is made in his image. The Christian message is a message of reason. No doctrine is laid down without a reason. Christ has told us to reason with our brother when he has offended us.[14] Peter reasoned with the Council of Jerusalem. We are told to love our neighbour, to do violence to no-one. So the Christian wants ways to settle disputes which are reasonable, not violent or arbitrary.

The principle of majority rule is not so easy to equate with specifically Christian doctrine. It is certainly wrong for a majority to impose its will regardless of the views of the minority. A more Christian principle is that of respect for minorities. In Northern Ireland, fifty years of majority rule by one party in the provincial government was brought to an end because, although it was elected on full universal suffrage, it was not thought to have given due consideration to the views and needs of the minority. Lord Salisbury, British prime minister at the turn of the century, thought that 'the right of the majority to impose its will on others' was 'a peculiarly dangerous threat to individual liberty, for the majority represented tyranny rendered confident by superior numbers'.[15]

So although Christians should obey government, Christians of a majority party in a democracy should not consider themselves entitled to ride roughshod over the views of the minority just because they have the right under democratic rule. And the doctrine of the popular mandate should not be interpreted to mean that the majority is not only entitled, but also obliged, to ride over the minority.

The Christian should be careful about the doctrines of populism. Governments can and should protect minorities. They cannot and should not abdicate this duty to the popular referendum. A referendum which is binding on government and cannot be set aside can show no discretion, no adaptability, cannot be altered or modified if the answer turns out to be exceptionally harsh and unfair. Nor can a popular majority alter the moral law to which governments must be accountable. Black is not white because a referendum says so. Evil is not good because it comes top of the poll. Governments must be responsible for all the people and must account to their Maker for all they do with the authority he has given them.

It is often assumed that autocracies are more effective than democracies. But this is not at all clear. All governments depend on consent and the government whose consent is based on popular election often feels far more capable of taking effective, if unpopular, action, than an autocracy which does not have popular support.

A distinguished American professor once tried to tell a European conference that it was difficult for a democratic government to contain inflation. It was at once pointed out to him that the military autocracies of South America had traditionally had a much higher rate of inflation. Someone else pointed out that the European dictatorships did no better than the democracies and that one country which had gone from democracy to dictatorship had multiplied its inflation rate by ten.

Economic historians, contrasting the wartime economies of Britain and Germany, have pointed out that the democratic government of Britain was able to mobilize its economy for war much more fully than the German dictatorship. Because the British government was elected by the people, it was able to call for greater sacrifices than a government which was not elected.

Party politics

Christians can accept very readily the principle of consent. What they find more difficult is the idea of party. The democracies have devised the system of alternative parties competing for power. It is a part of this system that the parties shall attack each other in public and each try to destroy the credibility of the other. For this reason almost all arguments are seen in party-political terms, and the public comes to discount what is said as one-sided argument. In some democracies most of public life is conducted in party terms, all senior public offices changing with the party. The head of state is a party leader. In other democracies, the head of state is above party and all senior posts are divided into political appointments, which change with the party in power, and equivalent permanent appointments, which do not. America has the former system, Britain the latter.

Christians dislike the party conflict because it seems to them so divisive. They feel that the government should aim to unite. It should govern for *all* the country and not just for their own supporters. Christians do join political parties and stand for office, but they seldom join in the attacks on their opponents with any relish. If there were another way to political responsibility, they would welcome it. They feel justified, in an imperfect world, in joining a political party which puts roughly the views they hold and they also feel justified in accepting the compromises and disciplines of party politics. But Christians have also been strong advocates of community government in Northern Ireland, and if a political system could be devised where power came more explicitly from the centre, which encouraged community government and discouraged faction, then most Christians would favour it over the rule of the bare majority.

In a society which discounts religion, there is a danger that party dogma takes the place of religion and demands from its followers a moral loyalty and condemns its opponents as moral outlaws. So long as there is political liberty, the party dogmas can be questioned. The greatest danger of dictatorship is that the party in power cannot

83

always be right and isolates itself by force and fear from healthy criticism.

The difference between a dictatorship and a democracy is not so much that the dictatorship does not allow for an alternative government, but that there is no non-partisan establishment debate. Everything must accord with party lines. The party line does not prevent debate altogether – it can be detected by expert observers – but it does effectively smother debate. The introduction of a monolithic party ideology leaves no forum for discussion. The press, radio and television are censored. There are no clubs. All meetings have to take place where they can be supervised. Genuine discussion opens up only in the depths of the forest.

It may be said that Christianity, too, is an ideology. But Christianity, unlike the current ideologies of Marxism or nationalism, is about ends and not means. It does not lay down a particular doctrine of government or economics. It says what society should be like as a result of good government, not what government itself should be like. So it has few political dogmas to enforce. There must be government and in secular affairs it must be obeyed – no more. A Christian may suggest political solutions, but he does not dogmatize – at any rate not on Christian grounds. And Christianity, unlike Marxism or nationalism, is not a divisive creed. It tells us to love all people, bourgeoisie as well as workers, expatriates as well as nationals. Christianity does not have to erect the barriers to defend itself against those to whom it is politically hostile. For it is not politically hostile to anyone. It wants to win those who oppose it by persuasion and it does not despair of influencing anyone, however hostile. Christianity does not seek to suppress opposing views. It prefers to answer them, as Christ did.

The Christian should be less susceptible to political dogma, should always keep an open mind, should always remember that he might be wrong. There is also tremendous value in putting views up for public debate. The Christian, above everyone, should respect the views of others, and should never be so arrogant as to believe that he, or his friends, have the sum total of human wisdom. In an autocracy, the fresh air of new ideas cannot penetrate the stuffy,

84

confined discussion of the ruling cliques. Mistakes are never admitted; error is enshrined as policy and any change is difficult in an atmosphere of fear and distrust.

The contribution of 'the establishment' and its limitations

The merit of a free society is that, in contrast to an autocracy, it can bring into the debate articulate, intelligent and informed people outside parliament and government who are prepared to advise from their specialist experience, debate the major issues in private and to give a lead in public. Included in this group, commonly known as 'the establishment', are the civil servants, trades unions, industrial and professional leaders, the universities, the television, radio and newspaper journalists and writers and well-known figures in local communities.

British civil servants in Northern Ireland during direct rule found that one of the problems of government was the absence of any positive support from the natural leaders of the community. The people to whom government would normally look in the rest of the United Kingdom to establish the general consensus were non-committal. They did not want to be involved. The moderate centre preferred to stick to its domestic concerns. Business kept going while politics ground to a halt. Thoughtful businessmen acknowledged that they were wrong, that they had left politics too much to the professional politician, that they had asked for favours but had given nothing in return.

Every government depends to some extent on a social 'establishment'. It is the link between governors and governed. In a materialistic society it is principally concerned with the industrial and commercial establishment. But there is also an establishment in the arts, in the great professions – in medicine, in teaching, in law – and a regional establishment in every major city and province. They are not 'the powers that be', but they are the people whose consent is very necessary to good government. The incoming Conservative government in Britain in 1970 was accused of dispensing for a time with the customary consultation with the trades unions. As one trades unionist complained, 'You'd have thought they would have recognized a vested interest when they saw one.' But the establishment is not just a vested interest. It has a positive supportive role. The difference between a *coup d'état* and a revolution is that the one retains the establishment and the other sweeps it away. It is because a revolution destroys this vital link between itself and the social organization of the country that it is forced to be so arbitrary in government. Until they have built their own establishment, their own bridge between themselves and society, they can impose their will only by force and fear.

Anyone who wants to reform society sees the establishment as an obstacle to progress. 'If only we did not have to consult them, how much faster we could get on.' But this is an illusion. If you want to make permanent progress you have to change people's minds. If you want to do this, you have to change the minds first of those whose opinions are respected. This means that you have to master the subject, to meet legitimate objections, to amend your proposals to make them workable and practicable. One young minister was determined to force his new legislation through against the opposition of an indignant establishment. An old civil servant was asked what would happen. He said, 'The act will become law and the government will not be able to operate it.' That is exactly what did happen.

The more complex society becomes, the more necessary it is to have this establishment bridge. Most legislation today affects some complex mechanism of society. Party manifestos are very general documents. The problems arise not in deciding what the party wants to achieve, but in framing legislation which makes sure that this is what is actually achieved and that there is not some unforeseen and disastrous side effect.

Government needs both expert advice and general support. The establishment gives expert advice and, in so far as the citizens respect this expert advice, it is in the position of giving general support. The temptation of the establishment is to trade its support for favours. An establishment is as capable of becoming corrupt as any other part of society. If it represents a very powerful interest, capital or labour, it may begin to insist that unless the government is run to its dictates, vital capital or vital labour will not be forthcoming to support the country's needs.

Wise governments try to organize the establishment in some formal way, to give it explicit responsibility. In the old days of agricultural societies this was done through an upper house with representatives of the landed interests. More recently it has been done through organizations like Britain's National Economic Development Council. But the real source of wealth in a knowledge-based society is neither capital nor labour (which have always existed) but the knowledge of how to make both capital and labour a hundred times more productive than ever they have been before. The organization of this knowledge lies with the universities and the great professions which dedicate themselves to teaching it and above all to improving it. Governments look increasingly to universities for support and advice. Academics have had great influence in Washington. In the Ulster troubles, the Queen's University, Belfast, was always able to provide reliable, impartial figures and their advice could be trusted by all parties. It may well be that the organization of this kind of advice on a more systematic basis, combining the universities and the professions, could give a much-needed keel to popular government and keep it on a straighter course through the shifting winds of opinion and the gales of partisan propaganda.

If the arguments of the establishment fail to carry conviction, then it is impotent – and rightly so. A nation's establishment depends on trust. It must be trusted by government and people to know what it is talking about and to be impartial rather than self-seeking. It has to be believed. Once an establishment figure is suspected of abusing this trust to press for partisan policies or for his own interests, then not only does he lose this trust, but he does great damage to the whole idea of public trust. If a Christian sits somewhat uneasily to party politics, then, by contrast, he should be particularly well qualified to gain a reputation for impartial and expert advice, the position symbolized by Joseph in Egypt or Daniel in Babylon and Medo-Persia.

The ultimate protection of government against undue influence by the establishment is that the establishment possesses only influence and government possesses final power.

Notes

1. Mark 12:17.   2. Matthew 26:52.   3. 1 Peter 2:13f.
4. Romans 13:1–7.   5. Acts 4:18–20.   6. Luke 23:22–24.
7. Acts 12:1, 2.   8. See Acts 24:26.
9. This is not the generally accepted view today. Revolution is the popular cause, especially if it is a long way from home and involvement goes no further than writing cheques. This is dealt with more fully in *Is Revolution Change?* (Inter-Varsity Press, 1972) to which I contributed, with Brian Griffiths (who edited the book), Alan Kreider of the United States, René Padilla of Argentina and Samuel Escobar of Peru.

Dietrich Bonhoeffer, who was executed by the German government in the closing days of the 1939–1945 war, is usually considered to have exercised legitimate Christian opposition to a tyrannical government. But the excellent and most sympathetic biography by his friend Eberhard Bethge (*Dietrich Bonhoeffer*, Collins, 1970) makes it clear that he entered into the plot against Hitler's life as a member of an influential Prussian family and not as a Christian pastor. It was for that that he was executed and not for his Christian faith. See Appendix B, pp. 102ff.

10. Matthew 19:8; similarly Mark 10:4ff.   11. 2 Thessalonians 3:10.
12. Colossians 4:1.   13. 1 Timothy 3:1–13; Titus 1:5–9.
14. Matthew 18:15; Luke 17:3.
15. Quoted by Lord David Cecil in his history of the Cecil family, *The Cecils of Hatfield House* (Constable, 1973), p. 242.

5 The nation

Nationalism: the new religion

When is national loyalty a virtue and when is it a vice? Is race part
of the natural order, and is the mixing of races against the divine
purpose? Are peoples right to seek independence in ethnic nationhood, or are the wars of independence a waste of human life? Are
people right to feel a special loyalty to the soil of their forefathers?
Should the Jews go back to Israel, the Ulster Scot to the mainland?
Should the Germans be reunited?

These are not theoretical questions; they are burning issues.
People live for them and die for them. Nationalism is the religion
of the twentieth century, more potent and more dangerous than
Marxism because it is a religion of the heart and not of the head.
When, in 1941, Germany attacked Russia, and Britain had to choose
to fight with the Russian Marxists or the German nationalists,
though the latter hoped that we might join their crusade against
Marxism we sided unhesitatingly with the Russians. Almost all the
wars in this century have had nationalism at their root – the Boer
War, the two German wars, Kenya, Cyprus, Aden, Ulster, have all
been about nationalism. Imperialism is dead; nationhood is the
popular cause.

But is it a cause to which the Christian can commit himself wholeheartedly? Is there Christian teaching on nationalism? What would
our Lord do today?

Perhaps it is best to start with our Lord's actions in his own day.

There was an intense nationalism among the Jews. They were God's very own people. He had promised a deliverer. Yet they were a subject race of the Roman Empire, and surely God would give them their independence again. They searched the prophets and were convinced that the imperial rule would be ended and that the Gentiles would cease to desecrate the holy city. If ever there was a case for nationalism, surely it was the case of God's chosen people. Yet Jesus turned his back on that case. He was not interested in Jewish nationalism. He paid taxes to the Empire and told the Jews to do the same.[1] When the Pharisees and Herodians set a trap for him he refused to speak against the Roman rule.[2] He refused to take up arms. When arrested, he told Peter to sheathe his sword.[3] He told Pilate, 'My kingdom is not of this world: if my kingdom were of this world, then would my servants fight.'[4] The Jews out of jealousy brought forward trumped-up charges that he was perverting the nation, forbidding the payment of tribute to Caesar and making himself out to be a king. Pilate saw through their motives and refused to convict him of nationalism.[5]

The apostles whom Christ appointed also turned their backs on the nationalist case. They had the full measure of natural feeling. Peter needed a vision before he preached to the Gentiles.[6] Paul longed for the conversion of the Jews,[7] yet he was obedient to the command to preach to the Gentiles and laid it down that in Christ Jesus there was neither Greek nor Jew.[8] The Christian church broke down all the barriers of nationalism.

The first millennium of the Christian faith saw the development of 'Christendom' out of the ruins of the Roman Empire and the invasion of the savage northern tribes. The Christians had a mission to the barbarian too. They tried to win the northern races, and what eventually emerged was the common bond of 'Christendom' transcending their fierce tribal loyalties. The eventual institutions embodying this idea, the Holy Roman Empire and the medieval papacy, were often far from Christian. But the spirit of Christianity was a unifying force, and, in so far as it had any influence over the principalities and power which took its name, it was to make them realize that there was more to life than tribal loyalty. The idea of Christendom, though abused, was a real political force.

In the Europe of the Reformation, John Knox ministered in England, Germany and Switzerland as well as in Scotland. Erasmus was as much at home in one country as in another. The English channel was a high road and not a barrier. There were no passports.

As Christianity declined in the countries of Christendom, nationalism increased. The cross gave way to the flag, and in one country after another the nation demanded an emotional commitment and loyalty which had previously been reserved for the faith. Yet at the very time when nationalism was demanding men's loyalty in Europe, the Christian missionary movement was growing most vigorously. Outside Europe Christianity spread to Africa and Asia and the church encircled the globe transcending, for the first time, every barrier of nationality and culture. But now the nationalist movement has spread too, and we find it dominating political thought and action in most of Africa and southern Asia.

The church in Nazi Germany

We see then that in the twentieth century nationalism has grown stronger and the church has grown weaker. In Germany the church was almost overwhelmed by nationalism. From the studies of the relations between church and state in that country between the wars, it is apparent that the reason for the church's lack of resistance to National Socialism was the tremendous appeal of German nationalism to the German Christians. It was only when the logical outworking of this nationalism began to appear that a few of the church leaders began to see where their true loyalty lay.[9]

The German churches were divided into Christians who felt that politics were no concern of theirs and those who positively welcomed Hitler's arrival in power. It is odd to remember that even the fearless Pastor Niemöller sent Hitler a cable of congratulations. Christians wanted a return to law and order. They were anxious about the moral state of their country and they were afraid of a communist revolution. They knew that Christians in Russia had

had a terrible time after the 1917 revolution and, nearer home, they had seen the brief communist régime in Hungary. Also, and most regrettably, they shared the average German's anti-Semitic prejudice, and their patriotism was too near to the strident nationalism of the Nazis. By the time that men such as Pastor Niemöller had realized their terrible mistake, it was too late. A united church might have stopped Hitler in his tracks; but, once in power, he edged the church slowly but surely back into the cloisters, supporting those who were still prepared to support him and isolating the minority, such as Niemöller, who refused to compromise their Christian position.

The German Jew, the first target of this nationalist and racialist movement, had lived in the country for centuries. He was not always easy to distinguish from the so-called Aryan. He had the same culture and held some of the highest positions in universities and public service. Those who blame the German church and imagine that it could not happen in their country need to reflect on the greater vulnerability of those parts of their immigrant population who are first or second generation, whose colour makes them easily distinguishable, whose culture is different and who do not hold high and influential positions.

In the 1920s the Germans lived in a democracy with freedom of speech. But they did not use that freedom of speech to condemn the rising nationalism and racialism of the day. The violence against innocent people and against the Jews in particular was wrong and should have been roundly condemned. Initially this was not a political but a moral issue, and one on which Christians had clear teaching. They were, of course, frightened of the communists, who wore their anti-Christian badge openly on their sleeves. The National Socialist party was not international or pro-Russian; it was strongly German and they were Germans. National Socialism promised to protect them from the communists. It promised a moral resurgence and they wanted a moral resurgence. It promised to throw over the Versailles Treaty, the consequences of which they suffered along with every other German. It promised strong rule, and after the economic chaos of the twenties they felt the need for strong rule. It blamed the Jews for most of their ills, and many Jews, with their international connections, had come through the slump better than most other Germans. So, carried by the tide of contemporary opinion, some Christians favoured the National Socialists and some Christians did nothing.

The period of National Socialist rule is particularly interesting because the Germans' complete defeat in 1945 put all the state documents into the hands of the victors and they were, therefore, available for study. It now appears that even a little protest from the Christian public would have gone a very long way. Hitler was as responsive to public opinion as any other politician. His authority did not rest on the solid base of an over-all electoral majority. He was extremely anxious to present a public front of national unity and he was very conscious that he could not do this if he roused the opposition of the churches. So he treated the churches gingerly at first, concurrently conditioning them, dividing off the more difficult sections and reducing their freedom of action.

Hitler's definition of religious activity was narrow. It was confined within the doors of the church and even there nothing was to be said of a political character. The definition of political pronouncements was widely drawn. By the time the churches realized what was happening, it was too late. The net had been drawn and they were caught. Yet they need not have been caught. Even then Hitler would not allow the pagan wing of the party to attack the religious side of church life and impose their own ideology on the country. He never repudiated his own membership of the church. He imprisoned only a small number of pastors and even those were treated fairly mildly. Dietrich Bonhoeffer perished in 1945, not for any religious activity but for joining the attempt by the German army to assassinate the upstart Chancellor who was ruining their country. Bonhoeffer is not commemorated as a martyr by the German churches.[10]

The German churches were ineffective between the wars, not because it was impossible to alter popular opinion or to stop Hitler in his tracks, but because the church itself reflected the popular mood which was sweeping the country.

Christians cannot escape their obligations as citizens.[11] If we follow the quietist tradition of non-involvement (which was strong in Germany), if we have doubts about the authority of the faith (which the German higher-critical movement had certainly encouraged), then we will be unable to help when our fellow citizens most need the support of Christian authority. It takes time to formulate a Christian view of events. It takes even longer if there is a preliminary argument as to whether there should be a Christian view. If we leave it until the crisis comes, there will not be time and we may be overtaken by events, just as surely as the German churches were.

The German churches were probably the only force which could have stopped Hitler. The liberal intellectuals were swept aside by strong popular feeling. The communists were in a minority and to the majority of Germans they represented a threat. But the churches had deep roots in Germany. They were organized. They were articulate. They covered the country – and they still spoke to men's consciences. The organized strength of the church is a great temptation. It has attracted worldly men who have used it for their own ends. But there are times when a movement of Christian opinion is all that stands between a country and moral disaster, when the strong appeal has to be made to the consciences of our fellow citizens. At that point Christian opinion must be formed and its impact must be felt.

John S. Conway in his excellent book on *The Nazi Persecution of the Churches, 1933–1945* reaches the following conclusions:

The Nazis' campaign would never have achieved the success it did if the estrangement of millions from the faith of the church had not already revealed a fatal weakening of Christianity. . . .

The church was unprepared and unsuited to cope with the situation. . . .

Four factors may be held to be chiefly responsible for the churches' meagre resistance to Nazi oppression. First was the ingrained tradition of pietism. The tendency of many Christians to limit their religious loyalties to the narrow goal of personal redemption had undoubtedly led to sincere and devout lives and has inspired the successive waves of missionary movements. But their failure to carry their Christian principles into political life had opened the way for a dangerous subjectivism which drew from its Reformation background the belief that 'politics do not concern the church' and an almost Manichaean conviction that the affairs of political and social life are irredeemable. Secondly, there was the characteristic German readiness to accept the existing political order without criticism and to exact obedience to established authority. Thirdly, there was the Nazi call for a renewal of the nation and revival of its spiritual life. But the so-called Christian principles of the 'German Christian' were wholly superficial and their fallacies were quickly exposed. By rejecting theological study in favour of 'positive Christianity' many of its adherents produced nothing more than thinly disguised apologies for their political ambitions clothed in the garments of righteousness. Finally, there was the churches' basically conservative outlook, which led them to accept without question the claim of Nazism to be the only alternative to communism. In their distrust of left-wing tendencies they had carried with them the bulk of their middle-class supporters, but no prophylactics had been taken against the challenge of the 'radical right' which advocated authoritarian principles, proclaimed itself fervent in its devotion to Christianity – especially as opposed to Judaism.[12]

Nationalism today

Nationalism and racialism are still with us, and there is a real danger that, without Christian debate, Christians will take their own opinions from the flow of popular opinion on nationalism. They are not cut off from the world. They have the same anxieties and fears; they read the same papers; they talk to their friends at work and next door. Unless they subject the opinions they form to the discipline of Christian debate, they will not see the dangerous paths down which the popular mood is leading.

A Christian lady was once waxing eloquent on the need to keep the British race pure. Her husband thought this funny and pointed out that, since he was a Pole, their joint contribution of two daughters had not helped much towards the purity of the race. She was thinking only of colour, but her principle was that of purity of race and she had not thought through the consequences of her views. Another Christian, a member of Parliament, was much troubled about purity of race. He could not bring himself to think that it was right to mix the races but could not find any Christian teaching on which to base this view. If these issues are not brought to the bar of Christian teaching they will do untold harm to the good name of the Christian church and will also prevent the church from fulfilling its functions as the light of the world and the salt of the earth.

Nationalism is not the same as patriotism. We can be patriotic without becoming excited about it. A patriot will do his duty when his country calls him. He will fight if his country is attacked; he will do a spell in public service if his government asks him. But nationalism is more in the nature of a religion. Nationalism is exclusive for it deliberately sets out to exclude other races from the body politic. It is your nation against all others.

German imperialism died in 1918. French imperialism died in Algeria and there followed a period of strong assertion of French national identity. British imperialism also died in the 1950s and, when it did, Britain was economically weak from the effort of sustaining a world position for so long, and managed to find room in the European Community only on hard terms. These are the conditions in which countries are driven in on themselves and are tempted to reassert their identity in strongly nationalistic terms. Already the smaller nations within the United Kingdom have begun to assert their national identity far more aggressively than ever before. It is easy to imagine some charismatic figure gaining enormous support in a drive for British unity. It could well be associated with a strong royalist movement, and those who have had to debate with the 'loyalist' movements in Ulster know that the expressed wishes of the monarch have little effect on such movements. Prince Philip warned of the dangers of nationalism in a public discussion in Edinburgh in August 1973, and it would obviously pose severe problems for a constitutional monarch. But, above all, it would pose problems for the Christian church. Most Christians want to be patriotic and loyal and, as Ulster has shown, it is extremely difficult, without a clear understanding of the Christian principle involved, to show the dividing line between patriotism and nationalism. But there is a dividing line and it must be drawn plainly and understood clearly.

The 'powers that be' are, of course, ordained of God and we owe them the duty of obedience as the Christians did in the days when Paul wrote to the Romans and Peter wrote his general Letter. But when the 'powers that be' demand the allegiance which can be given only to God, then we say with Peter, 'Whether it is right . . . to listen to you rather than to God, you must judge.'[13] The problem of government is to command allegiance. The less they can command it by appeal to Christian duty, the more they search for some other basis of loyalty. Nationalism is such a basis. But the transfer of the grounds of obedience from Christian duty to national loyalty is a dangerous transfer. Christian duty commands us to love our neighbour too – and the neighbour of the Jew was the Samaritan, not just other Jews. Duty to the 'powers that be' is not an exclusive duty; it is not totalitarian. Obedience to that duty does not excuse us from all other duties.

Of course, not all national feeling divides us from our fellow men. There is much that is good in loyalty and national feeling. In a world made uncertain and dangerous through sin and mistrust, it is natural that groups of people should band together for self-defence. It is much easier to govern those who have a common interest than those whose interests seem to conflict, and to get consent from those who are close to their rulers than from those who are distant. The less the degree of duty felt by the citizen, the more difficult the role of government. Dr Johnson may have said 'Patriotism is the last refuge of a scoundrel', but it is surely right that citizens should take a pride in their collective achievements. It is when patriotism is used to divert people's minds and to divide that it becomes dangerous.

And there is a very positive side to nationalism. Each group of people has developed its own culture, its own peculiar contribution to the life of mankind. The culture of a nation is surely a divine gift. God has not made the universe in a dull monochrome. He has made every kind of plant and animal in a profuse and fascinating variety, and mankind in the most fascinating variety of all. Within God's church we are all parts of the same spiritual body, but with different and complementary gifts. God surely formed his natural creation on the same basis. Language, poetry, literature, art, music, architecture and style of life differ from nation to nation. The world would certainly be a duller place if this were not so. When we travel we resent any trend to uniformity and we delight in the distinctive culture of the nations we visit. If Florence is overrun by strangers, it is no longer Florence. Peking is to build a skyscraper hotel, and we wonder whether the flavour of the 'forbidden city' will ever be the same again. Translators' English is not the same as Shakespeare's mother tongue. If the Scot lost his ruggedness, the Chinese his courtesy, the German his orderliness, the Spaniard his pride and the Welshman his eloquence, the world would be the poorer. But to try to retain the Welsh language by opposing the pervasive influence of BBC English is not the same as demanding self-government with threats of violence.

The multi-racial community

It is perfectly possible to have a multi-racial state in which the various nations are protected and their identity preserved. The United Kingdom has long been a state of four races – English, Irish, Scots and Welsh. Although the English have been numerically the largest race, all the other races have contributed their fair share to the life of the country. Indeed, the union has now lasted so long that the four original races are now strongly intertwined by marriage, friendship and cross-residence, so that separatism seems not only absurd but also impracticable. On top of the four original races, Britain has received exiles over the years from all kinds of countries. The Jewish community dates from Cromwell, the French Huguenots from the early eighteenth century. In this century we have had West Indians, Pakistanis and Indians, all with their separate cultures.

There are two ways of treating a multi-racial community. One is the American idea of the melting-pot, where all the races become one American people and an 'American way of life' supersedes the national culture. The other is the Canadian – and British – which accepts the cultural distinction within the multi-racial state. Toronto is a multi-racial community, yet neither the Jews nor the Scots have lost their national culture. They are all Canadian citizens with equal rights and duties, but they can still make their own distinctive contribution to their country's life.

Another country which has been immensely successful in bringing different races under federal rule is Switzerland. It has, including Romansh, four different languages. Yet it is one of the best-ruled countries in the world.

The biggest exercise in ethnic nationalism has been the Versailles Treaty following the First World War. Four defeated empires, Russia, Germany, Austro-Hungary and Turkey were carved up to form more than a dozen small and separate countries. Southern Ireland was at the same time separated from the United Kingdom and a Jewish national state was founded in Palestine. It was the beginning of the end of the multi-racial ideal of Christendom and an acceptance that the forces of nationalism were so strong that it was no longer possible for countries to be effectively governed except by those of their own race who could govern by appeals to nationalistic ideals. This process, now known as Balkanization, may seem the easy way out in a restless world which is unable to compromise or accommodate with neighbours who are genetically different. But nationalism is a false god. Because it contains the idea of separatism, there is no end to its divisive effect. Croats, for instance, were taken from Austro-Hungary and given to Yugoslavia; but although Yugoslavia is a union of Slavs and is a viable state, it contains six separate Slavonic races. Some of these, especially the Croats, retained their nationalism within the new state.

Another piece of the Austrian Empire, Czechoslovakia, itself came to grief on the problem of the German minority in Sudentenland. Eventually all of the Austrian Empire, except for the metropolitan territory, escaped from the shambling Hapsburg autocracy only to find themselves under a much tougher communist autocracy. We cannot say that the break-up of multi-racial communities under pressure has been a self-evident success.

Zionism

The most controversial issue for the Christian is Jewish nationalism. We are bound to believe that God will keep the Jews a separate people until the end of time because he has promised that 'all Israel will be saved'.[14] But that does not promise the revival of a territorial nation.

And if the Old Testament promises can have both spiritual and material interpretations, then it does not justify the use of force to reconquer the territory of the ancient kingdoms from those who have lived there for so long. The heresy which launched the medieval crusades should not be allowed to rise again in another form. 'My kingdom is not of this world: if my kingdom were of this world, then would my servants fight, . . . but now is my kingdom not from hence.'[15] If God is to restore territorial sovereignty to Christian Israel, he will do it in his own way. To quote an Old Testament prophet: 'Not by might, nor by power, but by my Spirit, says the Lord of hosts.'[16]

This is not to be unsympathetic to the Jews. At a time when multi-racial empires were suspect and every race was closing ranks, the temptation for the Jews to found their own territorial nation state was considerable. After the loss of six million Jews in the Nazi terror, the pressure was overwhelming. Great emotional sympathy goes out to a small beleaguered people, to David fighting Goliath. But we can still ask whether Zionism was right, even for the Jew.

Not every Jew is a Zionist. Many Jews feel that the establishment of a Jewish state which can hold only a fraction of the total Jewish race makes life much more difficult for Jews who are citizens of other countries and who are thoroughly integrated into the life of those countries. While there was no Jewish homeland no-one could talk of 'sending all the Jews back to where they belong'. They were accepted as British, Canadian, American, Brazilian or Dutch citizens of a particular religion or race. Nationalism bred anti-Semitism and anti-Semitism bred Jewish nationalism. It seems to be a vicious circle which can be broken only by whole-hearted advocacy of the multi-racial state.

In 1969 I shared a rail sleeper across Germany with a Coventry schoolmaster on his way to Czechoslovakia. On his previous visit he had met an old veteran who had been mobilized in 1914 to fight for the Austrian Empire against the Russians. He was captured and then put in the Czech national brigade to fight for the Russians against the Austrians. When, after the Revolution, the Czech brigade finally got home he found that the Versailles ethnic division had made him a Pole and he was called up to fight for the Poles against the Russians. In 1939 he was again called up into the Polish army to fight the Germans. His home town was then annexed, on ethnic grounds, by the puppet state of Slovakia and he was called up by the Germans to fight the Russians. He was once more captured and forced again into a Czech national brigade to fight the Germans. He rode home with the Czech brigade and had lived in peace ever since.

Empires have their faults, but the Balkanization of Versailles and the ethnic nationalism of our age can have some very stupid results too, and have a divisiveness which is far from Christian.

Notes

1. Matthew 17:24–27. Jesus paid taxes for Peter and himself.
2. Matthew 22:15–22.   3. Matthew 26:52; John 18:11.
4. John 18:36, AV.
5. Luke 23:4–14; John 18:38; 19:4, 6. Pilate gave way only when they brought political pressure to bear (John 19:12). He got his own back, however, by having the description 'The King of the Jews' fixed to the cross and refusing to alter it when requested to do so by the embarrassed Jewish leaders (John 19:19–22).
6. Acts 10.   7. Romans 9:1.   8. Colossians 3:11.
9. One of the best works on the relation between the state and church in Nazi Germany is J. S. Conway's *The Nazi Persecution of the Churches, 1933–1945* (Weidenfeld & Nicolson, 1968) on which I have drawn heavily for this chapter. There is a great deal of literature on the mechanics of the Nazi climb to power, but little that gives satisfactorily the reasons for their widespread popular support. To attribute it to a particular evil in the German character is to answer in nationalist terms and to assume complacently that it could not happen in Britain, Canada or America. Conway gives what few political accounts give, the reason for the crumbling of the Christian ethic and why it was important to halt the Nazi ideology before 1933.

10. See Appendix B, 'The background to Bonhoeffer's execution', below.
11. I have developed this theme more fully in *The Christian Citizen* (Hodder & Stoughton, 1969).
12. J. S. Conway, *The Nazi Persecution of the Churches, 1933–1945*, pp. 334f.
13. Acts 4:19.   14. Romans 11:26.   15. John 18:36, AV.
16. Zechariah 4:6.

Appendix B: The background to Bonhoeffer's execution

In his biography of Bonhoeffer (see above, p. 88, note 9) Eberhard Bethge writes: 'For a pastor, Bonhoeffer had unusual connections. His father was on familiar terms with Sauerbach, who was often able to bring along fresh news from the party hierarchy; his mother cultivated the family relationship with her cousin Paul von Hase (executed after the attempted coup of 20th July) when he was military commander of Berlin. Klaus (his brother) had contacts with the lawyer Josef Wirmer, the industrialist Walter Bauer . . . and with Otto John and Prince Louis Ferdinand. But in these crucial years, no one was nearer to him than his brother-in-law Hans von Dohnanyi . . . On 25th August 1939 Dohnanyi had taken on the duties of "Sonderfuhrer" on Admiral Carnaris' staff . . . he acted as a kind of private secretary to Carnaris. He was now fairly settled in the centre of . . . the conspiracy' (pp. 528–529). 'Dohnanyi confided in no one more than Dietrich Bonhoeffer . . . Dohnanyi introduced him relatively early to the narrower circle of conspirators' (p. 530). 'They started from the assumption that the army could not submit to Hitler's defamatory encroachments . . . the "resistance" would in future have to become a military plot' (p. 532).

'The third main section of the German resistance movement includes Bonhoeffer's actual complicity in the plot against Hitler . . . In each of these three stages, Bonhoeffer's participation and involvement in the events is considerably increased' (p. 628).

'The plan matured to assassinate Hitler on his anticipated visit to the front' (p. 684). This attempt failed, as did one on 21st March. 'A fortnight later Bonhoeffer, Dohnanyi and his wife and Joseph Müller were arrested' (p. 685). 'The Gestapo itself did not know what it had achieved by the arrests of 5th April – the smashing of the conspiracy's centre of activity. It was many months before everything was covered up and a new organizing centre created for the work needed for the Putsch' (p. 686).

'After he had become connected with that "conspiracy", Bonhoeffer assumed that his church would no longer be able to use him, once the facts came to light ... And he knew why his Confessing Church refused to place him in the Intercession Lists ... He sacrificed his professional reputation in the church and in theology' (p. 700). 'Why all this had to happen ... on this there is surprisingly little to be found in Bonhoeffer's papers from prison ... Why should he justify himself when there was no competent forum to address?' (p. 733).

The cover-up lasted almost two years, during which Bonhoeffer's famous *Letters and Papers from Prison* were written.

'It was only in the last month of the war, when Carnaris' whole diary was discovered, that an enraged Hitler had all the people who had not yet been tried condemned by a swiftly set-up field court of the SS and executed on 9th April (Carnaris, Oster, Dohnanyi, Bonhoeffer, Gehre, Strunct, Sact)' (p. 827).

'Bonhoeffer's own church ... made ... a strict distinction between Christian martyrdom and political resistance ... In a pastoral instruction on the first anniversary of 20th July 1944 (the final attempted assassination) it presented Paul Schneider to its congregations "as a martyr in the full sense of the word" and did not mention Bonhoeffer's name, but said it could never approve the conspiracy ... "whatever the intention behind it might have been."' 'A similar view was taken by those Bielfeld pastors who appealed to the Bonhoeffer family to protest against the naming of streets after Paul Schneider and Dietrich Bonhoeffer "because we don't want the names of our colleagues, who are killed for their faith, lumped together with political martyrs"' (p. 834).

6 Economic order

Conservation and economic development

The Christian believes that the universe and its natural resources have been created for the benefit of mankind. But it is clear from the commands given to Adam, and later to Noah, that we are only trustees. So no one generation may abuse its trust by taking out more than it puts in. On the contrary, Christ's parables of the talents and the pounds teach that each generation must put in more than it takes out. At the minimum we must replenish its resources, but ideally we must improve on them. The parables of the pounds and the talents call on those to whom God has given talents to multiply them. The man in each parable who buried his gift is condemned in the most severe terms.

The dawning realization that the mineral resources of the earth are being rapidly used up has led to a very powerful conservation movement with which the Christian must have a great deal of sympathy. We have no right to deprive future generations of irreplaceable reserves of energy and we have no right to do permanent damage to the earth's ecological balance. It used to be thought that man's scientific knowledge was the ultimate source of wisdom. It is now recognized, more humbly, that the creation is finely balanced and that we tamper with this balance at our peril. The Christian believes that God has created this balance and must support all efforts to maintain it. The deserts and dustbowls of the world, the bare mountains whose precious soil has been eroded, are a silent witness to the neglect of previous generations.

But the Christian's attitude must not be passive. It is not good enough for the conservationist who lives comfortably in an advanced industrial economy to decree that all economic growth shall cease at the point at which he himself has enough. This is to ignore completely the needs of the poor and deprived in his own country and more especially to forget that the majority of the human race is just above the starvation line, one step ahead of disaster.

Some conservationists are also inclined to believe that all economic development is extravagant of natural resources, inexorably crunching up reserves of minerals and energy at an ever-increasing rate. This is just not true. It is possible, as our knowledge of nature grows, to do far more with the same or even with less material. Growth can also conserve resources.

Aluminium, for instance, has a protective coating which minimizes corrosion, gives a far longer life than steel and is, therefore, much less wasteful. A large proportion of aluminium production is collected as scrap, re-melted and used again. It is easier to re-use than either steel or plastics. It is much lighter in vehicles than either wood or steel so its use gives large savings in scarce fuel. Most aluminium smelters use water-power which had previously been running to waste in remote parts of the world. The great post-war expansion of the world's aluminium industry has probably contributed to the conservation of resources, even though there is a fraction less of the original raw material – bauxite – than there was thirty years ago.

Even the development of the car has led to much lower fuel consumption for the same output of useful energy, and most engines today are designed to be more effective in their use of energy than engines manufactured forty or fifty years ago. Most house-heating systems are far more effective today than the old open coal fire where most of the heat disappeared up the chimney. A great deal of the electronics industry is resource-saving. Miniaturized circuits have transformed the radio from a massive instrument needing two men to move it to a tiny instrument held in one hand. The calculations now made possible by the computer and its aids reduce the use of resources in everything from goods tied up in warehouses to the weight of materials in bridges.

Another growth industry, pharmaceuticals, keeps the human body much more effective and has greatly reduced the loss of life and energy from illness and accident. In many countries some diseases have been eliminated altogether.

Other industries, like civil engineering, make an enormous contribution to the increase in the natural resources available to mankind. The Dutch civil engineers have reclaimed vast areas of sea. The Italians have tapped the tremendous hydro-electric power in the Alps. All over the world great dams have made the desert blossom like a rose. Roads driven into inaccessible regions have helped to bring bush-land into cultivation. Motorways have made drastic cuts in fuel consumption. Sewage farms and water-purification plants have reduced disease and re-cycled waste.

The cumulative effect of all these savings can be seen in the difference between import and export prices which, except in the rare-commodity boom, have favoured the industrial countries as they consistently increased their output with a lower and lower proportion of raw material input.

So it is possible to have higher living standards without an unacceptable increase in the use of scarce resources. We know far more than ever before of the physical universe and the means of harnessing its energy and improving its fruitfulness. The problem is that so much of the new knowledge is theoretical. A few skilled people, knowing exactly what they are after, can produce results in controlled laboratory conditions. But we lack the ability to apply this knowledge on the kind of scale needed to make an impact on the real needs of the world.

The most appalling waster of human and material resources is not industrial expansion, but war. A great deal of industrial output is productive. Most capital goods are bought for the improvement they will make in the productive yield of the manufacturing process. And there is some limit to human consumption. But war is utterly destructive. Enormous resources, energy, effort and skill are put into the production of armaments on both sides which are then blown to pieces. War is the ultimate extravagance. It is all input and no output. And it can easily destroy the industrial and agricultural systems on which whole populations depend for their very existence. When Albert Einstein was asked about the weapons of the next war, he said he was not sure, 'but the next war after that will be fought with stones'.

The industrial countries of the world are all based on high-consumption economies. In view of Christ's frequent warnings to the rich[1] and his concern for the poor, most Christians think it right to condemn excessive consumption. Non-Christian conservationists, too, are very vocal about it, but are not always very constructive when it comes to spelling out precisely how high consumption should be curtailed.

Too often the conservationists are people who have suddenly become aware that the rising affluence of the worker is making life a lot more crowded for the higher-paid. Their quiet suburbs are surrounded by new subsidized houses. The once quiet roads are jammed with workers going to work by car and the juggernauts which now feed the massive new shopping centres. The exclusiveness of air travel has given way to the crowds going on package tours and the whole of the service and distribution industry is now geared, not to the higher-paid member of one of the professions, but to the affluent worker.

The conservationist argument is too negative. As a working man was once heard to mutter, 'It's all right if you've got something to conserve.' Christ cared for the poor, and the Christian should be the last person to tell the poor that they have enough. Redistribution is inadequate and in an imperfect world there comes a point beyond which it is counter-productive. The only real help to the thousands of millions in the world near the starvation line is a vast improvement in the productivity of the earth's natural resources.

This kind of breakthrough was made after the Reformation by the countries which adopted the Protestant ethic of restraint in consumption, hard work, innovation and mutual trust. The Protestant ethic has been best expounded by the German sociologist

Max Weber, the leading British socialist Professor R. H. Tawney, and the present Master of Balliol College, Oxford, Christopher Hill. Their views are summarized in an appendix to my *The Christian in Industrial Society*,[2] and the body of that book outlines the Christian theology which leads to this very high degree of self-motivation.

The theology is not very complex. But it is in sharp contrast to the practice in most of the world today. The first necessity is a plain, straightforward honesty. In much of the world today the largest single obstacle to economic progress is corruption. Too many businessmen in too many countries tend to assume that the ten per cents all along the line are just like a value-added tax under another name. But they are not, for the tax is legal and certain, and graft is illegal and uncertain. Its main effect is to destroy trust and to make it extremely difficult to operate anything other than a family business – where the family bond ensures trust – or a foreign business, where head office does not tolerate graft. If university professors can be bought, who can trust the skill of a degree qualification? If technical advisers can be bought, who can trust their advice? If purchasing officers can be bought, who will delegate the purchasing duties in the business? If foreign-aid officials can be bought, who can be certain that the aid goes to the right people; and if it does not, what is the point of giving aid? If judges can be bought, who wants to conclude a difficult contract? And if government can be bought, how can the whole clogging, cloying process ever be brought to an end? It is the ability of men to trust each other which enables industry and commerce to be developed on a scale which makes an economic breakthrough possible.

The second ingredient is the belief in innovation, the belief that the world was made for man, is given to him in trust and that he must use his God-given talents to make the very best use of its natural resources.

The third ingredient is the restraint on personal consumption, which throws up a surplus which can be invested.

If the Protestant ethic is taken up in developing countries which adopt the Christian faith, there is no reason why it should not lead to the same economic take-off as it did in the countries which originally adopted the ethic.

As a result of this combination, the Christian is likely to earn more, to save more, to invest more, to improve his skill more and to be more trusted with authority and with other people's money. It is small wonder that it was the countries in which this ethic was preached which pulled themselves up by their bootstraps and, as they invested their surplus wealth around the world, pulled others up after them. It is this frame of mind and code of behaviour which is now at risk in all those countries – Britain, Scandinavia, Holland, Germany, Switzerland, Canada and the United States – in which it was first born.

The free-market economy has many faults, but the state capitalism of the socialist countries seems to have worse faults,[3] and the feudalism of many developing nations is perhaps the most corrupt and hopeless system of all. Certainly none of the current systems measures up to Christian standards. Yet, given Christian standards, almost any economic system might be made to work. It is not so much the system that really matters as the personal standards which individuals bring to the system. In the end people may well get the system they deserve.

To the individual caught up in a vast industrial machine this may all seem rather remote. Life has become much more complex in the twentieth century. Labour and capital have now become highly organized. How can the simple Christian code of behaviour make any difference in the world of the International Monetary Fund, the European Commission, the Organization for Economic Co-operation and Development, the world of the vast, multi-national corporations and of militant organized labour?

But officials of these great organizations say that they are utterly dependent in all they do on a continued spirit of goodwill and trust. Behind many of the international organizations the reality of life has been the wealth and goodwill of the United States. And in that great democracy at least part of the feeling of care for others must have come from the strong Christian community. From the time of the Marshall Plan until the Vietnam war, America felt a strong moral obligation to strengthen the economic life of the rest of the world. American money poured into the devastated countries of Europe. American money helped to rebuild Japan, to finance the International Monetary Fund and the developing countries through the World Bank. And although all generosity has mixed motives, and the recipients were always suspicious of 'Coca Colanization', there was an underlying strain of genuine duty to the rest of mankind. It is when goodwill falters that the problems begin. It is when patience with partners finally snaps, when war diverts resources from aid, when government is no longer trusted even by its own supporters, when principle gives way to *real-politik*, that we realize how far the foundations of economic prosperity rested on the goodwill of one great and generous country. No amount of international mechanism can make up for the failure of goodwill.

The same is true in Europe. The European Commissioners and their Directors-General repeatedly point out that the whole structure of the European Community rests on goodwill. They remind us that the veto of one country is still enough to destroy any proposal. Even in a crisis it is difficult to ask some countries to make any sacrifice for the common good. The Commission rests on the support of national governments and these rest on the support of the parliaments who represent the mood of their countries. The institutions may try to lead, but they must, in the end, be governed by the mood of the people. If this is selfish, suspicious and ungenerous, the institutions cannot create the conditions of general prosperity out of the air.

Each nation state has the same problem. In Britain the National Economic Development Council brings together government, industry and commerce and trades unions with a powerful sub-structure of bodies for each major industry. But the issue underlying all the technical problems has always been whether the parties could trust each other and whether they could pass on any feeling of trust to their supporters. The parties keep on coming back to the moral issue – whether industry can have confidence in the promises of government; whether, if government keeps its promises, industry will deliver wage restraint and investment. But it is worth having the Council only so long as there is an underlying moral purpose and the possibility of mutual trust.

Shop-floor power

The most acute problem in our interdependent society today is the ability of any section to disrupt any other. The laws on monopoly and restrictive trades practice have effectively prevented any one company from holding other companies to ransom. And the lowering of trade barriers enables companies to import to overcome any artificial shortage created by a competitor. In America the Robinson Patman Acts expressly forbid any company to exploit its market position and the multi-national giant IBM has lost important law cases to small competitors. But there is no such bar to a similar action by a company's employees. When they withdraw their labour, they are officially in conflict with their employer. But when government has committed itself to full employment and is committed, therefore, to finance the inflation needed to maintain full employment, the employer is a paper tiger. In the great majority of cases he does not resist and the wage award is passed straight on as a price increase, so that, as British Prime Minister Harold Wilson once said, 'One man's wage increase is another man's price increase.' In practice, therefore, a demand for more money is a demand against the community and those most hurt are all the members of the community who cannot, or will not, enforce similar demands.

In an industrial country the ability to enforce wage demands is most unequal. Some strikes have immense and immediate economic repercussions and some have none. A strike which affects the country's power supplies brings widespread loss of employment in almost every other industry. A strike of schoolteachers has hardly any immediate effect. The Republic of Ireland carried on through a four-months' strike of bank officials. And the sick and old cannot strike. Nor will the army or the professions where people depend on their personal care. Within a company a strike of any group astride the production line is likely to cost twenty to thirty times the amount of any settlement. So the pressure exerted by production workers can be dramatically effective. But a strike of cleaners or clerks has nothing like the same effect.

So there is a tremendous pressure on the employer to buy off strikes which halt his production process, dry up his cash flow and halt the delivery of goods vital to the production process of his key customers. This phenomenon is known as 'shop-floor power' and its economic effect as 'cost-push inflation'. It has the practical effect of diverting income from those without shop-floor power to those who can exercise it. The broad result is to lower the real incomes of the pensioners, the disabled, the service industries, the public services and the professions, and the income from savings, and to increase the real incomes[4] of production workers and the real wealth of owners of property which keeps its real value in inflation.

In the majority of industrial countries the damage to the less powerful sections of the community was avoided in the fifties and sixties by an unprecedented rate of economic growth, financed initially by American investment and then maintained by favourable trading arrangements and avoidance of the foreign-exchange burdens of defence. In Germany and Japan the high annual wage increases were paid for almost entirely by increases in productivity; in the other countries of the European Community and in Canada and Australia there was a slight inflation. Britain and America bore the heavy exchange costs of external defence and the exchange costs of overseas investment, so their income growth was slower and their rate of industrial disputes – perhaps as a consequence – was higher. Britain, being less self-sufficient in raw materials, suffered more, but as the rate of industrial growth collapsed in the early seventies and cost-push inflation continued, all the industrial world suffered from severe inflation.

At its root, this is a moral problem, the exploitation of bargaining power. This is the sin of usury. We are meant to use our strength to help our fellow citizens and not to exploit them. As applied to the Jewish smallholder by the Mosaic law, it was a command to help one's neighbour when his seed corn ran out and not to hold him to ransom by lending him seed corn at rates of interest which he could not possibly repay. Put simply, the temptation was to use your surplus to exploit his scarcity and make him so indebted that he had to turn over part or all of his land.

When the shop steward asks why he should not exploit his bargaining power to the full, why he should settle for less than the maximum he can get, the answer is that his neighbour does not have the same bargaining power and when prices go up to meet the wage increase, his neighbour will be worse off.

The shop steward's standard reply is that he does not see why he should hold back while there are other people who are richer than he is. This is as good a formula for passing the buck as any other. But as a real answer it does not bear examination. The very rich – as opposed to those with higher earned incomes – can benefit as much from inflation as the more powerful workers. They are seldom found advocating price control or wage control. They are usually in favour of the maximum freedom of the market and normally have the best advice on how to minimize taxation and keep the real value of their fortunes intact. They feel no sense of urgency to limit their freedom of action. And many of them are not under the jurisdiction of national governments. When the oil-producing states decided that the rate of inflation was too high, they limited production, preferring to keep their wealth as oil in the ground instead of as money in the bank. If we cannot take steps to control inflation before the sheiks give up their Cadillacs or the film stars give up their diamonds, we may well wait for ever.

The shop steward then points out that managers earn more than workers and that he will moderate his claims when the incomes are evened up. This too is unrealistic. If all surtaxed incomes were redistributed to the workers, it would give each worker only a fraction of his current annual wage increase. It is also wrong in principle that professional workers who work for longer hours between the ages of 15 and 25 and receive far less income during that time should not receive more for their resulting skill when they ultimately qualify. And it is wrong in principle that those who carry heavy responsibilities should not earn more for those responsibilities. They may be highly paid, but they are also highly expendable. A top executive is expected by his own personal exertions to earn for the enterprise – workers, shareholders and customers – five to ten times his direct cost to the company. It is the unprecedented expansion in productivity since the war which has produced the tremendous rise in living standards in the industrial world. This has depended on the skill and very hard work of the professionals in charge of the industrial machine. Their earnings have not increased in proportion and relatively their position is a good deal worse.

A country gets the industrial and commercial leadership, the civil service, armed services and legal and other professional services it is prepared to pay for. In those countries which do not pay enough the judiciary, the civil service and the police are corrupt, the army is a constant threat to government and industry is restricted and feudal. A Christian social order tries to inspire the best in human nature, but it also keeps a wary eye on the temptations to evil and does not make these larger than can be helped. 'You shall not muzzle an ox when it treads out the grain' is in both Old and New Testaments.[5] It is wise, if nothing else, to see that those who administer justice, or who care for other people's money and are responsible for the jobs and standards of living of thousands of workers, should not be forced to spend too much time in supplementing their official incomes.

There are today – as there always have been in the past – those who try to rationalize a new-found source of power. Production work is dull and professional work is interesting, so it is only right that the worker should exercise this new-found power to see that he is paid more for his dull and dirty job than the professional man for his clean and interesting job. But whatever the appeal of this rationalization it would be almost impossible to apply within any organization with a unified wage structure. Engineers who take the responsibility for making sure that an aeroplane actually flies or that a bridge actually stands up will not accept that they should be paid less than a man whose responsibility is limited to bending steel or cutting aluminium to an exact schedule of instructions. They, too, have to work on the shop-floor and on the construction site. And is a dentist's job less boring or more agreeable than the job of a long-distance driver?

But, in so far as the professional job is more interesting it is so because it is creative, because it is expanding the frontiers of knowledge, making possible and then making economic what was not possible or not viable before. It is professional skill which is at the heart of all our attempts to make two blades of grass grow where one grew before, to improve real wealth without wasting irreplaceable resources. To cease to reward the development of professional skill would hazard not only the material needs of the developed countries, but those of the developing countries who need all the surplus professional skill we can spare. And although people might continue for love rather than for money, fathers and mothers would discourage them, as they discourage their children today who want to go into professions such as acting or writing. Personal satisfaction does not shelter, clothe, feed and educate a family.

Before the war, and even for a time after it, trades-union leaders used to preach these moral truths to their shop stewards. It was not the object of trades unions to exploit their fellow workers. It was their purpose to use the bargaining strength of the strong to help the weak, to see that the railwayman in Wick was paid the same rate for the job as the man in Wolverhampton. The Christian teaching is that wages shall be 'just and equal' and this is broadly in line with the two trades-union objectives of 'the rate for the job' and 'parity'. Many early union officials were deacons in Methodist churches and the early Labour movement is said to owe much more to Methodism than to Marxism. The power of a capitalism which believed in the creed of the 'survival of the fittest' had to be met by the organization of the working man to maintain the Christian principle of the dignity of the individual. Christendom had abolished slavery, the Reformation led directly to political liberty, and, since political freedom and economic freedom must ultimately go together, it is not surprising that the countries in which the Reformation was strongest have also the strongest trades-union movements.

But 'shop-floor power' stands trades-union principles on their head. It uses the bargaining power of the strong to help the strong. It sheds crocodile tears for the weak, telling the government that it is responsible for pensions, but is determined to recover any tax increase needed for pensions by an equivalent wage increase, so that pensions can never catch up with prices. The trades-union leaders are not altogether powerless, but they are in grave difficulties. In the old days strikers required union backing to obtain strike pay from union funds. Today the union leaders are often not consulted and strikes are subsidized by welfare payments from the state to strikers' families and by income from secondary employment. There is a drop in income, but the community has decided that strikers shall not face the hardship of the twenties and the thirties. In the old days strikers needed solidarity with other union members. In the inter-dependent industry of today, the cost of a stoppage in one plant or even in a section of a plant is quite enough to bring the employers to heel without any aid from other union members. So if the trades-union leadership disagrees with the strike, it is left without any effective sanctions. An employer once complained about shop-floor militants to the General Secretary of the British Trades Union Congress. The reply was that, if the employers would concede to the official union what they conceded under threat to shop-floor militants, there would be stronger union leadership. The extremist political groups who exploit shop-floor power are not committed to a free society and have no stake in the present system of free collective bargaining. If it is destroyed, they are not the main losers and they have more chance to set up their own system which, to judge by eastern Europe, does not allow the same freedom to the individual. It is in their interests, therefore, to exploit shop-floor power and it is scarcely surprising that they do so, whatever the results for the lower-paid worker and pensioner.

In discussion of this point, the Trotskyites and Marxists say they disapprove of 'Stalinism' as much as they do of capitalism, but neither can point to a country in which their system operates. And although the Maoists can point to China, the Chinese system is not really open to inspection. By comparison the Soviet Union is fairly frank. I once received a delegation from the Soviet trades unions. After a long discussion on free collective bargaining, the formal vote of thanks was given by a very muscular lady representing the Georgian trades unions. She said, 'In Britain you have free collective bargaining. In Georgia we have other methods,' and presented a Georgian dagger as the rest of the delegation fell about laughing. Undoubtedly the Russian worker has devised 'other methods' to overcome the rigidities of the system – as has the Russian manager. But one is left with the impression that free collective bargaining on equal terms allows the greatest measure of freedom. It is the abuse of the system by those with temporary unequal power which is now endangering both freedom and full employment.

The Christian, by contrast, has a considerable stake in the present system, which contains much Christian idealism, and a great deal to lose if it is overthrown by authoritarian systems of left-wing, or, as is more likely, right-wing reaction. There is no obvious or easy political solution. The foundations of shop-floor power would be severely damaged by refusal to make welfare payments to unofficial strikers or by refusing to finance inflationary wage increases – even though this might push up unemployment to 10%. Both these would be very drastic measures. The one would certainly lead to some spectacular pictures in the press of starving wives and children. The other could create civil strife as it did when unemployment rose to this level among the coloured Americans and the Catholics in Northern Ireland. 10% of the population, with nothing to do and nothing to lose through riots, is a hazard to any community. Another political answer is to bring more of industry into the state sector so that shop-floor power is forced increasingly to take on the might of the state. Both these alternatives are most unattractive for those committed to peace, to personal freedom and to the rule of law.

The first need is to recognize the exploitation of shop-floor power for what it is, the moral issue of usury, the expropriation of the weak by the powerful. When people understand that they are not taking money from the employer, but from other workers, that one man's wage increase is another man's price increase and that some other men cannot afford it, then personal conscience backed by public conscience can exercise some restraint.[6] But until the moral issue is seen clearly, until people with power see that they must exercise it responsibly, we cannot go on to the next stage.

The next stage is to support the official union machinery, the machinery which was set up to spread the bargaining power of the weak over the strong. There are almost certainly more workers with Christian principles who care about the weak and want to preserve free trades unions than workers with political creeds who are prepared to exploit shop-floor power and do not mind the damage it does to the authority, the public standing and the ultimate freedom of their trades union. But the 5% with strong Christian principles need to turn up to meetings and see that the union leadership is elected on a poll which reflects their view.

The ultimate need is trades-union support for a fair wages policy, a policy in which differentials which are capable of agreement within the great bargaining groups of engineers, builders, miners and others are agreed between groups in one annual wage round. This would avoid the present leap-frogging and enable special cases to be recognized without opening the flood-gates to everyone who thinks that they have a similar case.

If it is argued that it is impossible to fix differentials between the traditional bargaining groups, then how is it possible to fix them within these bargaining groups, within companies, within nationalized industries, within the public service, the teaching professions, the hospitals and any other hierarchy with common bargaining? It is not a technical problem. A great deal of time and care already goes into the fixing of differentials. What is missing is the agreed machinery for fixing differentials which cross the boundaries of negotiating groups. Differentials within a plant can be fixed across trades-union boundaries; why not differentials outside the existing inter-union plant bargaining machinery?

Government and employers have to make up their minds whether they support the official trades-union movement or oppose it. Most experienced companies support it. Those who do not are frequently in trouble. Governments, sensing the public resentment of strikes and knowing that the public does not distinguish too clearly between union power and shop-floor power, have been tempted to curb the powers of the official union. But legislation, for instance against the closed shop, makes it much easier to form a breakaway union which can legitimize otherwise unofficial and unconstitutional strikes, or undermine a constitutional strike; and this, in turn, makes it more difficult for the larger union to retain its authority in calling and ending strikes.

Too often a government-imposed wage policy has seemed purely negative. It has been a short-term effort to stop inflation by decree. A fair wage policy must give price restraint as well as wage restraint. But no policy will succeed which does not seem fair; and no policy will seem fair unless it has machinery which deals carefully and systematically with differentials. Ideally this should not be a government body, but should be responsible to those who sit around the bargaining table, employee and employer as well as to government. Then they cannot disown it as they can disown a government body.

Without some such machinery it is difficult to implement the Christian principle of wages which are just and equal. But we now have a good deal of experience of the kind of wage-negotiating institutions which are needed in an economy with full employment, and we are beginning to know what will work and what will not. And just as the principle of the dignity and freedom of the individual has been embodied in parliamentary institutions in all those countries in the Reformed Christian tradition – and subsequently in many others – so the principle of wages which are just and equal also needs to be embodied in machinery which has checks and balances, which is sufficiently flexible to work in real life and which, like elected parliaments, carries the support of the vast majority as the best and fairest way of settling their differences.

Worker participation

Wage bargaining is not the only, or indeed the main, institutional problem in our economic society. As more people are literate and educated, as public affairs are freely discussed in the media so that most people can understand the issues, pressure has grown to make the organization of work more democratic and the control of working life more open to influence by those who actually have to do the work. Most people work for a limited-liability company whose ultimate control has remained exclusively with the owners. But the owners of most large companies are no longer identifiable. They buy and sell their shares like commodities, do not attend share-holders' meetings and show little interest in anything but the ac-counts and dividend. They have become, for the most part, absentee landlords; but they retain the power to sell control at any time it suits them without consulting either directors or employees. In practice directors have to look after the interests of employees and customers as well as shareholders, and though their legal account-ability as directors has been exclusively to shareholders, the more enlightened boards feel that the time has come to bring the legal position into line with reality and to recognize the wider responsi-bilities of the director.

Christian principles protect the rights of ownership. 'You shall not steal' is one of the Ten Commandments. But the general tone of divine law is that people matter more than possessions, and it is legitimate to ask how far possessions should confer power over people. Under the impact of Christianity, the absolute power of possession of one person over another was broken in Christendom. The feudal obligations to local lords did not survive in more settled conditions in society and after the Reformation they disappeared completely in Protestant countries. The industrial revolution grew haphazardly without any Christian philosophy of employment, but with the parallel growth of the power of the trades unions. The working man who found a better method of making a product was free to become an employer – and many did. If he had the organizing and technical skill to produce a better product, that gave him the ability to pay the wages and his justification was his economic ser-vice to the community. If he could not, he went out of business and his employees lost their jobs. Gradually this was developed into a philosophy. But the philosophy was never acceptable to organized labour, even though the effects were cushioned by government commitments to full employment, and it became less and less ac-ceptable as the small employer gave way to the great industrial companies, whose boards of directors were necessarily remote from the place of work. Organized labour argued that these concentrations of power must be accountable to the elected government.

Another philosophy was 'co-determination' and this attracted a great many adherents among thoughtful people outside the main camps of organized capital and organized labour. The principle of co-determination was especially influential in the 'scientific management' movement of the thirties. It was put into operation in West Germany after the Second World War, when there were no remaining vested interests and the social order was being rebuilt from the ground up. The method was a 'works council' representing the workers, and a supervisory board on which a third of the places were held by the workers' representatives and two-thirds by the owners. The supervisory board is responsible for the appointment and supervision of the executive board which runs the business. The success of German industry has been one of the wonders of the world. It is partly due to the effect of some remaining Protestant ethic on the discipline of the German people. It is also partly due to the massive aid given after the war and the continued inflow of foreign currency to the NATO armies stationed in Germany. It was helped by currency reform, the lowering of tariffs, and possibly by the backing which German capital gave to German industry. But it remains true that German labour relations have been far better than in any other major industrial country with organized labour, and there has been a marked absence of demarcation disputes and other signs of internal strife. No-one can say that the experiment has been a failure. For a quarter of a century it has been an evident success. The European Commission has suggested that all countries in the European Community should follow the German example and many have already done so in one form or another.

In Christian countries within the Reformed tradition, political power is accountable to those over whom it is exercised. In industrial society economic power is now almost as important as political power and it is probably right and wise to make that power accountable too.

The burdens on boards of directors are now very heavy and they really cannot be borne any longer in a continued atmosphere of institutionalized conflict. There has to be a single body with a unified responsibility for everyone immediately affected by company policy and performance, covering employees, shareholders and customers. The expansion of the boards' terms of reference to include this over-all responsibility, and the inclusion of employee representatives on the board who accept their over-all responsibility, produces a governing body with a collective responsibility to resolve differences. This must surely be a sound objective for Christians.

A public code of conduct for industry

It is not enough for powerful institutions to be accountable to those affected by their power; they must also be seen to operate by acceptable moral standards. Both the institutions themselves and those who operate them should have a code of conduct. On the initiative of St George's House, Windsor, a great deal of agreement has been reached by representatives of the Confederation of British Industry and the British Institute of Management on the need for both corporate and managerial codes of conduct.

The Confederation of British Industry stopped short of a declaration on the need for a corporate code of conduct only because the government declared that such a code would need legal sanction. The British Institute of Management have adopted a personal code of conduct for members with sanctions of the usual professional kind for breaches of the code.

The view of the BIM is that it is best to have a general code and rely on case law to fill out the details as time goes on. It may be that the best way to a corporate code is to ask leading companies to spell out and publish the code by which they actually operate. Most major companies do have such a code, but it is operated by unwritten consensus and the unwary discover it only when they do something which is not expressly prohibited, but which everyone is supposed to know should never be done.

Proposals for a management code of conduct were made to the International Congress of Management (CIOS) in Munich in the autumn of 1972. They were passed on to member movements and at the time of writing are due to be discussed again at the next triennial Congress in Caracas in the autumn of 1975. Similar proposals, made to the European Management Symposium (sponsored by the European Commission) in Davos in February 1973, resulted in the 'Davos Declaration' on the need for a professional code of management.

It is often argued that it is the competitive spirit and not codes of conduct which produces economic results. What is needed is an aggressive go-getting spirit, not a list of pious platitudes. It is certainly true that management must be dedicated to improvement, so both managerial and corporate codes should certainly contain a commitment to optimum economic performance. Management must be creative, inventive, innovative; not static and administrative. Competition is supposed to keep management on its toes and up to a point it does. But too often competition ensures the survival of the fattest rather than the survival of the fittest and the whole idea is Darwinian rather than Christian. Christianity is more positive. It looks to progress through action and not through mutual destruction, to co-operation rather than competition. It tries to heal the lame rather than kill them off. When a great firm such as Rolls Royce gets into difficulties, it is pointless to throw 8,000 skilled aeronautical engineers on to the labour market all at the same time when there is no other aeronautical firm to employ them. It is better to pay them to make aero-engines than pay them, through social security, to do nothing.

The threat of a take-over is little more constructive. In an informal National Economic Development Office[7] study of conglomerates, the two main factors to emerge were, first, that there was no economic case for the rash of mergers in the late sixties and, second, that most of the mergers were, in any case, defensive. They were put together by managements who knew each other and merged their companies so that the combined companies were too large to be swallowed by someone no-one liked. The experience of those who have had to manage companies after take-overs usually gives them a great respect for the old management. In one case their main mistake had been to make an investment which was so large that it depressed their share price and made them vulnerable to the bid before the investment had time to pay off.

There is no doubt, too, that take-overs, with their predatory flavour and their almost complete disregard for the interests of employees, make the worst possible climate for good labour relations. The directors of the companies taken over seem like puppets on a string. How can company managements encourage employees to identify their interests with those of the company when the managements can be displaced so swiftly? A new manager called the foremen together in a south Wales plant and gave them a run-down of his plans. One old hand said, 'I've heard fourteen managers talk like that, and when you've gone I'll still be here doing the job the way I've always done it.'

If shareholders are to have such power, they must also bear the corresponding responsibility. But it should be possible for the major institutional shareholders to organize themselves to take an active and constructive interest in the companies they collectively control and for companies to discuss major decisions with the responsible representatives of their major shareholders. If those decisions involve a temporary fall in the earnings they should be able to obtain some guarantee against the sale of institutional shares to a bidder taking advantage of a dip in the share price.

But a more permanent arrangement would be the granting of a charter to companies who had an acceptable corporate code of conduct, including the obligation to maximize economic performance for the benefit of shareholders, workers and customers. Companies would be entitled to retain the charter so long as it could be demonstrated that they had adhered to the code, including a better-than-average economic performance, and, while they did retain the charter, they should be immune from take-over. The award of charters should be controlled by the representatives of the management institutions, the trades unions and the government acting for itself and on behalf of the consumer. This seems far more likely to provide economic performance and the performance of social obligations than crude competitive capitalism. In that system economic survival demands that the pressure of shop-floor power is not resisted for too long, and day-to-day survival from the take-over bidder weighs too heavily in the balance against social obligations and long-term economic objectives.

Summary

It is not possible to say that these are definitely Christian solutions. Christian principles lay down ends, and Christianity leaves it to each succeeding generation to work out their own means of arriving at those ends. Paul did not condemn slavery directly in the Letter to Philemon, but the principles he gave to the Christian slave-owner were found, in a short time, to be incompatible with slavery and therefore with the economic system which depended on slavery. Christianity did not take slavery for granted and it does not take capitalism or Marxism for granted. If the systems fail to measure up to Christian standards of man's obligation to man, then Christians have to devise some system which does. The Christian is interested in the survival of all, not just the survival of the fittest company or the fittest social class. The application of the moral law to ancient Israel favoured the diffusion of their means of production – which was land – and condemned its aggregation into large units which reduced the majority of Israelites to hired hands. The application of the moral law today might do worse than follow similar principles in today's very different world.

An economic system which meets Christian principles should conserve natural resources, but must make continually improved use of what can be employed. It must encourage man to expand the frontiers of knowledge and to apply this new knowledge on the maximum scale to the good of all. Its organization of work must encourage creativity and innovation, for man was made in the image of God the Creator. It must use man to his full potential and not just as an unreliable extension of the machinery. Its organizations must respect the dignity and potential of each individual. They must be organized as teams of human beings. It must also guard against the worse side of human nature and recognize the possibilities of corruption, swindling and oppression. It must see that rewards are just and equal and that there is adequate and agreed machinery for the settlement of disputes. Economic organization is not a divine institution like the state. It is a voluntary organization of free men, so its leaders have only such sanction and recognition as they can obtain from their fellow men. It will always fall short of the highest Christian ideals; but all Christians should always try to adapt and reform it so that it conforms as closely as possible to those ideals in the economic conditions of their own generation.

Notes

1. See Matthew 19:16–26. But note that not every Christian is told to dispose of all his riches. Some are meant to be trustees; others to save for their children. The young man in question had 'great' riches which suggests that they were well in excess of any conceivable need. See also Matthew 13:22 with its warning of the way in which 'delight in riches' can choke the 'word of the kingdom', and the parables of the rich fool (Luke 12:16–21), and of the rich man and the beggar (Luke 16:19–31). The drift of all this teaching is plain. Riches bring care. There is always the temptation to rely on them and cling to them and to ignore the needs of the poor. And 90% of people in industrial countries today are as rich as the 'rich' in the Bible.

2. Inter-Varsity Press, 2nd edn., 1966.

3. This was certainly my impression when, as Director-General of Britain's National Economic Development Council, I discussed their problems with visiting delegations from eastern Europe.

4. An increase in 'real' income is the increase in income minus the increase in prices over the same time.

5. Deuteronomy 25:4, quoted in 1 Corinthians 9:9 and 1 Timothy 5:18.

6. When the state can no longer finance inflation because it has to borrow the money from foreigners, then six men's wage increase will equal one man's job as wage increases put the economy into brutal recession. The problem then will be to recreate the confidence needed to restore full employment.

7. The British National Economic Development Office, serving the tripartite Council. The findings of the study were read as a paper to the Economic Society at Exeter University.

7 Church order

Christians' love for each other

The church has a key position in the Christian social order. First of all it must teach the Christian faith; then its members must show their faith by their life. Christ taught that we should judge not just by what people say, but by what they do – 'You will know them by their fruits,'[1] and, 'By this all men will know that you are my disciples, if you have love for one another.'[2] If this love of Christians for each other is lacking, the church is dead. At its heart a church is people. The early churches met in each other's houses. It was these people and their bond with each other which formed the church.

A great deal of the instruction of the apostles to the churches is about this relationship of the members to each other. Very few of the matters which divide the churches today are given any space in the Letters. Forms of baptism, forms of worship, forms of government and formal relationships between churches are almost entirely ignored. There must be baptism, worship, government and relations to other churches. But the exact form of these matters much less than the love which inspires them. If love is lacking the form is worthless. To quarrel about form is futile, for the quarrel matters far more than the form. And so often the form is a matter of human preference on which the apostles say nothing at all.

The love Christians have for each other must cross all social and racial barriers. This truth makes a particular impact at any international conference of Christians where the delegates may come from democracies, military dictatorships and communist countries. Some have to go back to churches meeting under the most severe restraints. Some can talk freely only out in the open. Some are so poor that they cannot buy a coffee or pay for the cheapest excursion · without help. Yet Christians together are scarcely conscious of the differences. The unity of all these very different people in a common faith, the love of all these strangers for one another, the common worship in forty different tongues, are what stand out. Christianity is not a religion of the 'Christian' countries, but stretches across the whole world.

Those who advocate the racial separation of Christians on the grounds that God has put us all in separate races ignore the tremendous intermixing of races from one millennium to the next. The United States, Canada and Australia are all countries of mixed race. England is a polyglot of Celt, Anglo-Saxon, Dane, Norman, Scot, Jew, Huguenot and Pole as well as the more recent arrivals from Pakistan, Jamaica and Uganda. Where now is the Hittite, the Roman, the Goth, the Vandal? In Ulster mixed marriage between Celt and Scot has for long been almost impossible, but a little blurring of the edges between the communities would have done a power of good. No theory of racial purity can possibly hold against the clear message of Paul that there is no longer to be any barrier of race within the Christian church.[3]

Nor is there to be any barrier of wealth between Christians. James states in the most explicit terms that the rich are to have no special favours.[4] The setting aside of special seats for the local landowner in English parish churches was a concession to local custom quite contrary to James's plain teaching that to 'show partiality' to someone because of his position or wealth was to 'commit sin'. Neither he nor the other apostles would countenance dishonouring the poor in this way. Nor was the outward evidence of wealth to be flaunted in church. The only instruction on the exact form of the Lord's Supper was that it was to be same for rich and poor alike.[5] The only privilege of the rich was the privilege of giving to the work of the church.[6] God gave him his wealth for a purpose and he is not to use it selfishly or ostentatiously.

Wealth is still a terrible barrier within churches and between churches. It is probably not as bad as it used to be. In countries in which the church has been relatively strong there has been a great lessening of inequalities. It is difficult now to tell a person's income from their dress. No longer is there an Easter parade and no longer do the wealthy members of the church flaunt their new finery on Sunday. But there is now a geographical barrier between suburbs and the cities. There has been a great move by those who could afford it to rich one-class suburbs. The great cities are surrounded by new, flourishing and affluent churches, while in the inner cities the poor are left behind to share their gaunt crumbling buildings with the new immigrants. A few downtown churches still have a cross-section of society. Central London, for instance, still has a mixed community. But that is the exception.

The rich Christians are meant to look after the poorer church members and it is much more difficult to do this if they are not members of the same church. Physical proximity makes us care, but distance makes us careless. The elderly tend to be independent and will not have help forced on them. But can we really allow the old lady sitting along the pew to suffer when we could help her? Ought we to keep our homes to ourselves when our hospitality would mean so much to so many? And if we have a professional skill which others lack, ought we not to share with them the benefit of our knowledge?

One church had two elderly retired ladies living in a local-government flat. They were kept awake at night by the knocking of the antiquated heating pipes; yet despite their sleepless nights they could not bring themselves to move. Other members of the church helped them to make up their minds – they were in a terrible dither – and saw the local authority. As a result a new flat was provided, and church members looked after all the removal. But this flat was away from the bus route and overlooked a railway line, which made just as much noise as the pipes! So the church swung into operation again, calmed them down, saw the officials, got another flat, moved the furniture once more and at last saw them happily settled.

There is more to poverty than lack of money. A church is often an asylum for those who are mentally retarded and who find no companionship in the world outside. If the average church does not have more than its fair quota of mental cases, it is not doing its job. Some are beyond all reason. One church had an old lady some years ago, known as mad Annie, who believed very strongly that she was the Queen. Since the church was just past the Palace she was for ever arriving full of complaints that the guards and police would not let her into her own home. She was all right provided no-one argued with her. To those who were rash enough to do so she was apt to deliver a swift blow with her umbrella! But although some can be violent when crossed, most are lonely and depressed and simply want the human companionship which the church can give.

The modern cult of youth tends to divide young from old. But the church must have both. The exuberant spirits of the young can cheer the old and their vigour can help those too feeble to help themselves. But experience can also help youth. Many Christians will always remember the kindly elders in the church in which they were children, who were never unkind or unjust. They were wise men who, without at all pressing a point of view, had the ability to impart their wisdom to others. It is a great mistake for the old to fuss the young or to try to manage them. They should be there as a solid and secure background, ready to advise and help when asked, always available but never overbearing. They should try to set an example, in their marriages, in bringing up their children, in their relation to each other and in their relation to the world outside the church.

The church bridges the deep cleavages not only between different races and different ages, but also between different social groups. If a professional man meets a shop steward every Sunday in church, it is much more difficult for each of them to go away with the standard public image of the other. The professional, whose job isolates him from the working man, begins to realize the working man's fears and problems. He hears the views of the foreman and sees the image of the management from another point of view. And the shop steward has a better understanding of the skill of the professional and some idea of the contribution he makes from 9 a.m. to 5 p.m. apart from sitting in a warm office drinking coffee and tea. Of course, there are disagreements and arguments, but they are conducted with the mutual respect of those who like and trust each other and are not going to allow the differences in their work to come between their strong bond of Christian friendship.

It is difficult to see any other social organization which performs this function. Almost all other societies bring together people of similar tastes and background. But the Christian faith touches every-one – Matthew the tax-gatherer as well as Paul the Pharisee – and brings them all together. In the world the rich have one kind of club, the poor another; the young want one kind of entertainment and the old another; and different races notoriously band together in their different ghettos. The constitution of the Christian church tells it to cross all these barriers.

It is in this cohesive function that a church differs most from a 'movement'. For example, Christian movements for students are not churches. There are many young Christians who find them much more to their liking than a church because they cater very specifically for their needs. But although they are a great help they are no substitute for a church.[7]

The same is true of many evangelistic movements. Very often these can seem to produce much more spectacular results. They can touch those whom the church does not reach. They are not burdened by the historic differences between one church and another. If they wish they can take their campaigns anywhere into anyone's parish without consulting bishop or moderator. They can ride the crest of the latest fashion in worship and communications without consult-ing anyone on form or liturgy. But so many of them tend to appeal to one class of person rather than another. The Methodist movement eventually became a church. It did great good among the workers who had not been touched by the established churches. But it might have been better for the social cohesion of Britain had the established

churches been able to retain the Methodists, and it would undoubtedly have done the established churches great good.

Church discipline

There are still Christians who, in spite of what scripture says,[8] do
neglect the practice of meeting together. A few are addicted to
sermon-tasting, drifting without commitment from one church to
another, never satisfied that the ministry is quite good enough. But
a church is not a pulpit – it can survive without a minister – and
the command is clear. It is the positive duty of every Christian to
belong to a particular church and to put himself under the jurisdiction of its elders. Even the leader of the most successful Christian
movement must still be a member of a particular church, must still
put himself under the jurisdiction of others, must have some other
elder whose advice he is prepared to accept. If this population of well-
intentioned but drifting Christians could put their weight behind
the wheel of a particular Christian church they would do great good.[9]

The church is entitled to the attendance of its members. There is
nothing so encouraging as the sight of the whole church together in
one place, nothing more discouraging to a minister and the re-
mainder of the congregation than a half-empty building. And to the
outsider a semi-filled building is a semi-enthusiastic church.

The church is also entitled to our money. Although there is
nothing in the New Testament which specifically commands the
Christian to pay a tithe, Paul does ask the church at Corinth for a
proportion of their incomes as God has prospered them.[10] He does
not say what proportion; but since, in principle, the Christian is
told by Christ to exceed the law, the tithe should surely be the
minimum. And I see no reason why we should deduct state taxes
before arriving at our tithe. I know that in most countries today
taxes on income are progressive, the higher the income the higher
the percentage tax, and that top rates can be over 75%. But at a high
income surely the Christian can afford to give a much higher proportion of his net income? Spending beyond a certain level cuts us
off from members of the church who have much lower incomes. The

nature of the job may demand some differential and, in countries with a means test for student grants, a high gross income bars the children of that family from free higher education and so creates extra burdens. But the Christian should be sensitive to poorer members of the church, and a tithe on gross income and on realized capital gains removes the temptation to needless expenditure. It is those with low incomes, nearer to subsistence, who find the tithe a hardship. But often, as in the story of the widow's mite,[11] it is the poorest who are most faithful.

How can we expect the world to take notice of us when we keep our ministers in penury? The teaching elder, Paul tells us, is 'worthy of double honour'.[12] Although ministers may be reluctant to suggest that 'double honour' may be expressed in money, that seems to me to be the context of the statement. Yet today ministers often receive less than the average wage. If this interpretation is correct, the absolute minimum for any minister should be double the average wage in his community. And although he is provided with a manse or vicarage, that must be used for study and pastoral entertaining, and he still has to provide out of his income for a home for his old age. How can the Christian expect the church to be taken seriously when its paint is peeling, its hymn-books are dilapidated, its winter congregations huddle in overcoats, its plumbing is primitive and its minister cannot afford to buy his own books? Money does not buy a spiritual church, but financial generosity is evidence of a spiritual church. It is the visible evidence to every passer-by, and to everyone who drops in, that some people today think that the church is still worth while and that it deserves to flourish.

A church, unlike a movement, has to have a minimum hierarchy which has the power to exercise discipline. It has the power to admonish,[13] to rebuke[14] and finally, if all else fails, to expel.[15] This discipline helps the church by stiffening its standards of behaviour and ensuring that it does not come into disrepute. But it also helps society by bringing in some social discipline short of the law. Society could not exist if every dispute had to be brought to law. If society does not have the self-discipline of a moral creed, then it either degenerates or the state extends its power and individual freedom is progressively removed. Various groups in society can exercise a degree of internal discipline. But they are not set up for the purpose and have no comprehensive creed of their own which commands universal acceptance.[16]

This is the practical difference between humanism and Christianity. Even on the many matters where humanist and Christian agree, the humanist is not organized to deliver the necessary measure of consent in society. Most humanists would probably agree with the Christian on the need for wages which are 'just and equal'. But whereas there are Christian pulpits from which this principle can be preached up and down the country, there are no humanist pulpits. While nurses can and do consult their minister and elders on the morality of striking for more pay, there are no similar groups of humanists to consult. Newspapers may thunder at those with industrial muscle of capital or labour who hold their neighbours to ransom. But this does not carry the same individual weight as a warning word from a fellow Christian whose views we have respected for twenty years and who has a positive duty to exhort and warn all those who damage the good name of the church.

It is not too difficult to conclude the intellectual exercise of discovering the common good. It is somewhat more difficult to translate this into social institutions which command the assent of the established interests. The really difficult part of the exercise is to persuade those whose economic power could give them more that in social justice they should stand back in favour of others. It is at this point that society needs the help of moral guidance in local communities from those whose moral standing and judgment is widely accepted in their local community. And where the churches stand empty, whether in the big city or in a remote mining community, in a smart suburb or a ghetto, there is no common morality to bridge the gap and society slips into suspicion and confrontation.

The power of the church in society

How does a church make an impact on the community? As the real power of the church declines, the debate on the recovery of its power grows more intense. Everyone wants to use short cuts. All the techniques of modern communication are called in aid. One person can now address millions on television.[17] Radio, magazines, advertising, tapes and loudspeaker vans are all tried. But still the churches' influence declines. Then changes of style are introduced. Beat groups are brought into the cathedrals and the church identifies with the latest trends. Still the numbers go down. Then it is decided that it is the church buildings which put people off and that it is necessary to return to the house church. But that does not seem to turn the tide either.

The fact is that without spiritual power the church is not so different from any other social organization. It is the spiritual power which gives it its unique authenticity, which makes the impact, which brings the world to the church to find out what is going on. It is unnecessary for a church with spiritual power to seek the ear of the world; the world will be all ears. It was spiritual power which filled the churches at the Reformation and at the Puritan and Methodist revivals. It was spiritual power which filled Spurgeon's Tabernacle, and which brought into the churches the hundreds of thousands of converts in the missionary movement.

Christ has promised this power to his people. A universal revival may be exceptional, but the power of the Holy Spirit has been promised to all Christians: 'You shall receive power when the Holy Spirit has come upon you; and you shall be my witnesses in Jerusalem and in all Judea and Samaria and to the end of the earth.'[18] The early disciples could not themselves go to the end of the earth; but the church can and does. And the power of the Holy Spirit goes with us.

What is this power? It is the power to keep the divine law; not all at once and never perfectly, but a great deal better than before we were Christians. John says that 'if we say we have no sin, we deceive ourselves, and the truth is not in us'.[19] But if we are Christians we should not continue in sin[20] – in disobedience to the God who redeemed us and whom we profess to love.

And because we love God we should love the other members of his church. They may be ugly, boring, silly, tedious, depressive or quite mad. But they are our fellow Christians and we have to love them and care for them. The Spirit who is in us is also in them. Love is reciprocated. Christians are surrounded by others who really care for us. If we go away, they are glad to see us back. If we are ill, they are anxious. If someone in the family dies, they rally round. And they provide our children with a vast range of 'uncles' and 'aunts' who are concerned about them and a great number of 'cousins' with whom they can grow up. Loneliness is the curse of the modern world. The Christian should never be lonely, never left out. Those whose church is in a city or university town, who welcome a stream of visitors and students, have friends in all parts of the world. And even if Christians in other countries have never visited your own home church, they offer unrequited hospitality. There must be few cities in the world where a Christian could not find the warmest welcome to another Christian home. There are few Christian homes without room of some kind for a guest. So the church has the power of love.

The Christian is told to love his fellow Christian. But he is also told, in Christ's second great commandment, to love his neighbour as himself. The church must never be self-centred. Its membership should be closed to those who do not accept its spiritual authority over them. But its doors must always be open to everyone and it must always care for the community in which it lives. It must care, as Christ cared, for their bodies as well as their souls. It must care for the destitute, the orphan, the widow, the sick in body and mind and for the social outcast. It must love its enemies, do good to those who hate it and pray for those who abuse it.[21] It was this great care for the misery of humanity which brought the crowds flocking to Christ. He healed and taught, he taught and healed. He cared for their bodies and then he cared for their souls. He could not care for one without the other. Evil had harmed all parts of his creation and he wanted to put right all that had gone wrong.

There were some who followed only for what they could get. There were some who were healed and went away. But the leper who came back,[22] the man born blind whose faith confounded the Pharisees,[23] the paralysed man lowered through the roof[24] and many

others received healing in soul as well as body. So there will always
be 'rice Christians' as the Chinese called those who came to the
mission for the handout. But it does not matter. Christian love is
not conditional on spiritual results. Christ cared, and the Christian
must care too. Christ was patient, and the Christian must be patient
too.

The Christian church has a long record of social care. The relief
of poverty and the care of the sick have been the church's duty
throughout the centuries. It has been responsible too for the spread
of education and has founded schools and universities through
Europe and then throughout the world. Much of this has been taken
over by the state. But universal state welfare is open to abuse and
the abuse may bring it into disrepute. And education has a moral
base which sits uneasily in a secular educational system. In many
countries the state provides neither welfare nor education and the
care of the sick is still primitive. So there is still a place for the church
in welfare both to fill the gaps and as a backstop. And there is
especially a place for the church to bridge the gulf between the
developed countries and the underdeveloped. The average worker
in a developed country is rich in comparison with the average family
in Africa or Asia, many of whom do not have work and are on the
verge of starvation. Our duty for the poorer members of the church
is not confined to those in our own country. Paul's collections in
Greece were made for the poor Christians in Jerusalem,[25] and it is
surely a duty of the Christian church in prosperous countries to look
after those on the poverty line, not just by paying for missionaries
but by meeting some of the material needs of those who are in dis-
tress. The medical mission is one way of doing this. But perhaps
we should spend time and money on agricultural specialists and in
providing initial capital which will enable those without any resources at all to pull themselves up by their own efforts.[26] This
might avoid some of the pitfalls of government aid.

But a social gospel which makes the church nothing more than
a benevolent society is a denial of Christian truth. Christ taught as
he healed and his teaching set people by the ears. The social-
gospellers at the turn of the century abandoned the teaching of

Christian truth for a benevolent message which was little different from the views of liberal-minded men of the world. The church had no distinctive views of its own and no-one saw any need to pay further attention to it. And when the terrible slaughter of the First World War made the liberal views of life look utterly inadequate, most people left the churches altogether. So the church must be a vigorous witness to Christian faith. It is the power of the truth which makes men free.

By now it must be apparent to most Christians that the corrosive force of evil cannot be met except by the more powerful forces of good. It used to be said that evil was caused by poverty and lack of education. But there has never been more education and among the industrial nations there has never been more wealth more generally distributed. And all the indications of social instability show a strong trend for the worse. Crime is rising everywhere. The higher incomes rise, the more industrial discord seems to rise. War is held at bay only by the existence of the most terrifying array of weapons of mass destruction the world has ever known. Piracy has returned along with the very old business of kidnapping for ransom. The Utopia of the pragmatic, non-dogmatic liberal seems to have disappeared over the horizon for ever. It may have been preached from Christian pulpits. But it was never any part of Christian truth.

Christ taught that all men were subject to God's law. He said that he had come not to destroy the law but to fulfil it. The church must preach God's law too. Mankind resents the whole idea of divine law. We accept the need for law, but we want to make our own. We ourselves want to decide what is right and what is wrong. We prefer a world of relative values.

Against this, the Christian has to insist that all are subject to God's law and that we shall all be judged by it. The Christian message shows the truth about God and the way to God. So Christians have an absolute obligation to warn their own generation of the truth and to show them the way. The church has a prophetic function. It cannot remain silent. No matter how unpopular the message, it must be preached. Christ was persecuted for his message and he told us that we shall be persecuted too.[27] But the Christian church must hold and teach these absolute values, for they are the truth.

It may be unpopular to preach the truth, to proclaim that envy and greed are wrong, that adultery is wrong, that exploitation of the weak is wrong, that it is wrong to condemn the sins of others and ignore our own, that it is wrong to be indifferent to the poverty and suffering of those we could help, that it is wrong to tell lies – any sort of lie. But it is the duty of the church to preach all these things. It is especially the duty of the church to preach against the sins of its own generation, to run against the tide of fashionable opinion.

We must beware of those who say that the Christian message is old-fashioned. Eternal truth knows no fashion. That is not to say that the church should deliberately set out to be provocative – far from it. Christ taught in parables so that those who had a conscience could hear and those whose conscience was hardened could not pick on his words. His opponents felt terribly frustrated and were for ever urging him to be more explicit so that they could catch him in his words. But they failed. So Christians, too, must be wise, must not be offensive, must be ready, as Peter told us, to give a reason for the hope that is in us.[28]

Christians must put their message in love. We do not thunder anathemas at the world at large. We are not warning our enemies that they will receive their just deserts. We are warning our non-Christian friends, because they are our friends and because we care for them. It is a matter of real grief to us that they are blind to the truth, that they trust in their own intelligence, that they have no comfort in disaster, that, with all their charm and idealism, they are still so vulnerable to evil and, above all, that they have, in the end, no hope beyond the grave. So we try, in all we do, to set a standard which is Christian and different. We let them know that we are Christians. We try not to offend them by pressing our views on them, but we hope and pray that they will talk to us, that they can meet other Christians and especially those whose job it is to preach and teach. When, as so often happens, they become Christians, we do not feel that we have forced it on them, but that God has answered our prayers and that his Spirit has shown them the truth.

The preacher has a different task. He has to speak to those he does not know. It is easier for him to warn because the pulpit is impersonal. But every warning from the pulpit must be done in love. It must be clear to every stranger that the preacher and every member of the church care for his eternal soul. And the preacher must not only preach the law of God; he must also preach the gospel. God's justice in punishing evil goes together with his love in providing a way of salvation. He has come to earth as a man and borne the punishment of sin himself. To all who believe, he promises forgiveness. After the disastrous fire of Chicago in 1871, which resulted in so many lives being lost, D. L. Moody, the great American preacher, vowed that he would never again preach the law without also preaching the gospel. He had confined himself the Sunday before to an exposition of God's justice and judgment on sin, intending to deal with the way of salvation a week later. But a large part of his audience, who had heard the law and not the gospel, perished in the fire. Never again did he separate the two, never did he fail to conclude a message on God's justice without the message of God's love.[29]

The Christian church does not have to be perfect to make an impact on society. As the Letters show there was a great deal that was wrong in the church which turned the world upside down. But it has to have love and it has to have spiritual power. It is in the world and is a visible secular organization, but it is not 'of the world'.[30] It operates in the spiritual kingdom and it is the church's capacity to lay hold on the power of the Spirit which differentiates it so sharply from the world. People do not come to church to hear the parson say what the Sunday papers have already said with far more insight and erudition. They come for something different, something the world cannot give; and if they do not find it, they go away empty.

The power of the church depends heavily on prayer.

> The devil trembles when he sees
> The weakest saint upon his knees.

And well may he tremble, for God has not only taught us how to pray, but has also promised to answer prayer. He is sovereign, he is all-powerful and he has promised to use his power if we ask for it. We must not, as James says, 'ask wrongly, to spend it on your passions'.[31] We must ask in faith.[32] We must ask together with other Christians.[33] But whoever asks receives; whoever seeks finds.[34]

But it is especially in prayer for the salvation of others that Christians realize the power of prayer. Why should anyone change a whole life-style and become a new person? And why should that change coincide with our prayers? Those who discuss the change as an academic piece of psychology may find reasons which they think adequate. But those who have prayed for their friends, who have not pressed them or even persuaded them, and who have then found their prayers answered, believe that it was the result of spiritual power in answer to prayer. Churches often find that convert after convert has had, somewhere in the background, and sometimes unknown to him, an old aunt, a distant cousin, an old friend, a grandfather, praying that he will become a Christian.

So the church must get down on its knees and pray. It must pray for itself; for no church is faultless, and we do not always know the faults we have which take the savour from our salt. It must pray for kings and all who are in high positions,[35] and as it prays, it may sympathize a little more with the problems of government. And then it must pray for society, for the needs of our fellows, that they, too, will see themselves as they really are and that their conscience will be awakened to their desperate need. It must pray that God's will may be done on earth as it is done in heaven[36] and it must pray that he will use our church to save our own generation. And it must keep on praying because we 'ought always to pray and not lose heart'.[37] 'This kind never comes out except by prayer and fasting.'[38] Eventually the prayers of the church will be answered.

The wrong use of church power

In most societies today the church seems a failure. It has not failed completely and certainly it has not failed finally. But its salt has lost its savour and its light has lost its power. It makes very little impact, and so society has become confused and divided, looking for new gods and finding none to help it or save it. The churches today have become very like the churches of which the apostle John wrote in the book of the Revelation.[39] They have left their first love. They have allowed their leaders to lead them away from the true faith. They have become dead. They have little strength. They are luke-warm. They think they are rich, but they are poor. And yet, like those churches, they have some life left; they have had patience. Many of them have suffered for their faith and held fast to the truth, have served faithfully and are still able to strengthen what remains.

The world can and does also point to all the occasions when the organized church has supported worldly interest rather than social justice. People write letters to remind advocates of a Christian moral order that many bishops opposed the great Reform Bill of 1832, that the church has often been found on the side of the strong against the weak, the oppressor against the oppressed, the noble and the landlord against the peasant. They recall that there have been times when the church has been associated with torture and massacre and that it has often been no better, and sometimes even worse, than the worldly government to which they were meant to set an example. But this is to say no more than Christ and the apostles have said, that the church can fall into the hands of worldly people who will use it for their own worldly purposes. When this happens, it is no longer under the control of Christians. It has been captured by pirates.

Christ said that the kingdom of heaven was like a mustard seed which grew into a mighty tree into which all the birds of the air came to lodge.[40] Sometimes you can hardly see the tree for the lodgers and there have been times when you could hardly see the church of Christ for the worldly courtiers who held its offices and used it to damage their opponents. The apostle John warns of anti-Christian religion as well as anti-Christian government.

Because an effective church has great influence, it is a constant temptation to worldly people to take it over and use it for their purposes. The Bourbons used the French Protestants, the Huguenots, in order to seize power in France. But they changed to the Catholic faith to gain Paris, and when they were firmly entrenched they turned on the Huguenots and drove them into exile. In our own time, the opposing parties in Ireland have used religion to reinforce their political ambitions and, as a result, have done enormous damage to the good name of the Christian church.

Christ warned his disciples of the leaven of the Pharisees and Sadducees.[41] By leaven, as the Gospel tells us, he meant their doctrines. The teachings of the Pharisees were not the same as the doctrines of the Sadducees. The Pharisees added to the truth; the Sadducees took away from it. The Pharisees were ritualists; the Sadducees were interested in worldly power. The Pharisees believed in the after-life; the Sadducees were sceptics who did not believe in a resurrection. The Pharisees made all kinds of detailed laws for individual behaviour; the Sadducees were more anxious about securing the office of the high priest.

Today's Sadducees, in their anxiety to remain the official guardians of religion, are quite prepared to dispose of whole tracts of belief if these offend the spirit of the age. They explain that they are incompatible with advanced knowledge. They really mean that they are opposed to current opinion – which is much more important to those who are ambitious for high religious office. Advanced knowledge has nothing to say about the resurrection since it is outside the scope of its data. But modern opinion is against it and so are today's Sadducees. The state of the art of modern sociology is fairly fluid, but modern opinion is relativist, preferring 'situational ethics' to notions of absolute right and wrong, and so are the Sadducees. They are quite prepared, if need be, to deny the Ten Commandments, arguing that laws of this kind are necessary only for the primitive children of Israel wandering in Sinai. And if Christ himself endorsed them – indeed spelt out their implications more fully – that was only because he, too, was a child of his time. They are rather keen on the 'Jesus of history' not so much because they believe the history as because they can counter his views with 2,000 additional years of human wisdom.

If one is somewhat more sympathetic to the Pharisees, it is because they do not actively deny the faith. But adding to it has the effect of denying it. By making God's forgiveness depend on ritual, they deny the complete effectiveness of Christ's death in meeting God's justice. They substitute works for faith, in complete contradiction of the apostolic statement that 'no human being will be justified in his sight by works of the law'.[42] And in interposing the priesthood and the saints between Christ and the Christian, they contradict all that Christ and the apostles ever taught on prayer. In their detailed rules of worship and behaviour they bind on men burdens as heavy as the old Pharisees.[43] They lay down detailed rules for behaviour which Christ and the apostles never laid down.[44]

The right use of church power

The officers of the church have authority in the church and the traditions of the church (incorporating the practical experience of generations of saintly people) command respect. But the ultimate authority of the Christian church must be Christ, the head of the church, and the apostles whom he commissioned to teach the truth. If church leaders at any time put their own authority above that of Christ and repudiate by their actions the letter or the spirit of the apostolic teaching, then Christians must, in turn, repudiate them.

Many Christians feel that, because the power of the church and the power of the state are quite different, they should be visibly separate and that the jurisdiction of the church should be strictly spiritual. The governments of this world are also subject to moral authority. So the church, which sets the moral standards, cannot afford to place itself in dependence on those who might be tempted to change the standards to accommodate their own ambitions.

And yet the separation of the church and state can go too far. Governments which insist on a completely secular attitude to policy are in real difficulties when they run into a moral issue. They have no commonly accepted morality to which they can appeal. If they appeal to custom, they are called old-fashioned. If they appeal to common interests, they are on difficult ground if those interests change. How do you persuade one group in society that it is wrong to threaten or damage another group unless both groups have a commonly agreed moral code to which you can appeal? And how can a democratically elected government appeal to the supporters of the party which did not elect it if they have no common ground? How can there be limits to the conflict between parties without agreed rules which will hold hard under the acute stress of the struggle for supreme power?

It does not matter too much whether the state is officially Christian or is officially secular. America has so far done rather well as a secular state. But although it is a secular state in theory, it has a strong vein of Christian morality running through its establishment which has kept the ground rules of political debate. It is only now, when Christian morality is on the wane, that the rules have begun to be broken, that men in power have used any device available to ensure the retention of power. The crisis of Watergate was not a storm in a teacup. Amid all the tangle of tapes one clear theme emerged; who kept the conscience of the nation? If the head of the administration is tempted, on what grounds is he to be judged? There was a great deal of talk about ethics by the young men of the administration. But the ethics they discussed were made by men and could be adjusted by men. One professor may say it is wrong to counter subversion by subversion; but it is said that he does not know what it is like to accept ultimate responsibility for the security of the state. Thus have tyrants down the ages justified their exceptional powers. Christian morality judges subversion wrong whether it comes from the subject or the state. It is especially wrong for government, since it destroys the public trust on which government by consent is founded, and since the use of government power to damage political opponents destroys the confidence of opposition parties in the democratic system. In a democratic system there must be some common morality which is beyond argument. Almost all the democracies have had this background of accepted Christian morality. It is an open question how long democracy can remain if the Christian moral code is widely abandoned.

The more powerful the spiritual life of the church, the easier it is to have influence without power, to remain separate from the state and yet to give the state an accepted morality on which it can base its laws and administration. It is a weak church which needs an official position. It is a strong church which can keep the state at arm's length. So the contribution of the church to the community depends on its own spiritual power.

Notes

1. Matthew 7:16; see also Matthew 3:10; Luke 3:9.   2. John 13:35.

3. See Colossians 3:11; Galatians 3:28.   4. See James 2:1ff.

5. 1 Corinthians 11:21f., 'For in eating, each one goes ahead with his own meal, and one is hungry and another is drunk. What! Do you not have houses to eat and drink in? Or do you despise the church of God and humiliate those who have nothing?'

6. 1 Timothy 6:17–19, 'As for the rich in this world . . . they are to do good, to be rich in good deeds, liberal and generous, thus laying up for themselves a good foundation for the future, so that they may take hold of the life which is life indeed.'

7. M. C. Griffiths in his excellent and very practical discussion of the relevance of the church, *Cinderella with Amnesia* (Inter-Varsity Press, 1975), devotes a whole chapter to the church and the student.

8. Hebrews 10:25.

9. Too often Christians judge a church by what they can get out of it, not by what they can put into it. There is no point in attending a church where there is no teaching – we all need spiritual food; but we should settle to one teacher or another and exercise our rights as church members instead of voting with our feet.   10. 1 Corinthians 16:2.

11. Mark 12:41–44; Luke 21:1ff.

12. 1 Timothy 5:17. NEB translates, 'Elders who do well as leaders should be reckoned worthy of a double stipend.'

13. Titus 3:10; 1 Corinthians 4:14.

14. 1 Timothy 5:20; 2 Timothy 4:2; Titus 1:13; 2:15.

15. 1 Corinthians 5:13, 'Drive out the wicked person from among you.' But *cf.* 2 Corinthians 2:5–11 where Paul advises them that the person expelled, having repented, ought to be brought back.

16. Even the professional codes, which apply to a small minority in society, depend on prevailing morality.

17. Not that television and radio should be despised. Opportunities should certainly be used when offered, but they are no substitute for personal contact, for personal example, personal dialogue and pastoral teaching.

18. Acts 1:8.   19. 1 John 1:8.

20. 1 John 3:3, 'Every one who thus hopes in him purifies himself as he is pure.'   21. Matthew 5:44; Luke 6:28.

22. Luke 17:12–19, 'Were not ten cleansed? Where are the nine? Was no one found to return and give praise to God except this foreigner?' (verse 17).

23. John 9.   24. Mark 2:3–12.

25. Romans 15:26; 1 Corinthians 16:3.

26. This might be especially helpful to Christians in countries where the bribery is so pervasive that the Christian feels bound to exclude himself from most employment. Christian finance might enable Christians with qualifications and gifts to set up their own organizations and run them by their own standards.   27. John 15:18–20; cf. Luke 6:26.

28. See 1 Peter 3:15.

29. J. C. Pollock, Moody without Sankey (Hodder & Stoughton, 1966).

30. See John 17:14, 16; 1 John 2:16.   31. James 4:3.

32. James 1:6.   33. Matthew 18:19f.

34. Matthew 7:8; Luke 11:10.   35. 1 Timothy 2:1f.

36. Matthew 6:10.   37. Luke 18:1.

38. Matthew 17:21, RSV margin; Mark 9:29. Although prayer can be made at any time and in any place there are occasions when we must give ourselves to prayer.   39. Revelation 2 and 3.

40. Matthew 13:31f.; Mark 4:30ff.; Luke 13:18f.

41. Matthew 16:6; Mark 8:15; Luke 12:1.   42. Romans 3:20.

43. Matthew 23:4, 'They bind heavy burdens, hard to bear, and lay them on men's shoulders; but they themselves will not move them with their finger.'

44. This includes, in my view, the compulsory celibacy of the clergy, the banning of contraception, monastic vows and scales of penance.

8 Christian liberty

Everyone wants freedom. We seek it for ourselves as individuals. But all the great groupings of society are campaigning continually for freedom for their members. The unions want free collective bargaining. Management wants a free-market economy. Capitalists want freedom to move their money from one country to another to find the highest profits. But government wants to maintain its sovereignty, its freedom to govern on behalf of all the people, freedom to curb any sectional or individual interest which threatens the good of the community.

So one man's freedom can be another man's bondage. When people demand freedom they must ask, Freedom for whom, at whose expense? A free and civilized society must be based on strong self-discipline, reinforced by institutions which encourage conformity to that discipline. Most people agree that the basic freedoms are freedom from want, freedom from fear, freedom of speech and freedom of religious belief.

Freedom from want

Freedom from want demands a considerable redistribution of wealth and income in order to enlarge the freedom of the poor and underprivileged members of society. Redistribution is dependent on the self-discipline of those who pay taxes and on the power of government to encourage self-discipline. Never before in human society has so much money been raised for so many people with such little effort, and never before have such enormous transfers been made from rich to poor. Those who do not have the responsibility for engineering and policing this transfer are inclined to take it for granted, and those who want less government but greater economic equality are inclined to believe that the process can be extended indefinitely however complex the taxes or however resentful the taxpayer.[1]

If the great majority of taxpayers did not have a high standard of self-discipline, a willingness to curb their freedom in order to increase the freedom of the lower-paid, this movement from richer to poorer would be impossible. A very considerable apparatus of state is needed to make certain that those with a weak conscience stay in line. If, for instance, those earning more than £4000 a year in Britain were taxed at 100%, the average wage would be increased by only 4%. So the redistribution has to include the higher-paid worker, not just the very rich. If society is to achieve freedom from want, then all who earn more than the average wage have to exercise considerable discipline and curb their own freedom.

Freedom from fear

Only those who have lived with fear can know what it is really like. Sometimes fear arises because governments abuse their power so that rulers can remain in their high and powerful offices long after they have ceased to command the support of their country. But since even a tyrannical government cannot fight all the people, widespread fear probably comes more often from a breakdown of government than from an excess of it. The most recent breakdown in Britain has occurred in Northern Ireland. Whole areas of its two largest cities were unpoliced and private armies sprang up followed by private protection rackets. Prominent citizens were afraid to speak in public, would not be photographed and scarcely dared speak even to friends. There were private feuds and private executions. Innocent people were kidnapped, children were caught in crossfire, churchmen of either religion were threatened if they intervened and those who offended in minor ways were bound to lamp-posts, shaved, tarred and feathered. Innocent passers-by were blown to pieces. To the vast majority in Northern Ireland freedom means not the abolition of law and order but its restoration. To them anarchy means complete loss of freedom, and law and order a restoration of freedom.

To those who want the maximum personal freedom the police appear as oppressors rather than protectors. But those who want the curtailment of police power should consider whether this will produce freedom or whether it will produce private bodyguards and private armies. Although the Christian believes that human nature is idealistic and that everyone has a conscience, he also believes that human nature has a baser side which requires to be kept in restraint. If it is not kept in restraint, if the evil in society is allowed a free run, then it will curtail the freedom of all of us.[2]

The problem of peace kept by gangs or private armies is that their decisions are arbitrary and there is no court of appeal. Where there is a proper legal system, the police are subject to the courts and the minor courts are subject to the senior courts and all courts are subject to the rule of law. The gang and private army are subject to no-one but themselves and certainly are not subject to any appeal to the rule of law. Those who offend them are 'rubbed out' and their corruption, if not all-pervasive, at least pervades so far that no-one is certain who is on its pay-roll and who is not.

Freedom from fear requires trust between one person and another. But if we are to trust those we do not know, we must have an effective rule of law. If we find our trust is misplaced we can then take them to the law. But if we cannot trust the law, if the law is powerless, or corrupt, or at best uncertain, then we are not free to deal with those we do not know. Every individual transaction has to be protected and the whole basis of civilized social life and of economic life is undermined. It is small wonder that the great commercial capitals of the world are in the cities where the rule of law is strong and the courts are respected. And it is small wonder that countries where the rule of law is weak and the police are corrupt or powerless remain in perpetual poverty. A society gets the police and judicial system it is prepared to support and pay for. If it thinks they are not worth supporting, then there is a strong danger that private interests will support them for private ends. Then those who have been free from fear will discover rather sharply and too late what fear really is.

Freedom of speech

We hear a great deal today about the need for free speech, coupled with absolute opposition to censorship of any kind whatever. Since the Christian gospel is spread through preaching, the Christian above everyone believes in freedom of speech. Since we believe that our gospel is the truth we also believe that it will stand comparison with any point of view and we welcome free and open debate. No-one is more reluctant than the Christian to put the power of censorship in the hands of government.

And yet the Christian who believes in loving his neighbour is anxious to see that he is protected from hostile words as well as hostile acts. The Christian believes that God will judge people by words as well as deeds,[3] and that what people say can matter just as much as what they do.[4] So we should support laws against defamation of character. No-one must be robbed of his reputation or his standing in society by jealous or malignant words, and there must be some limit to our freedom to damage by what we say.

The Christian should also support laws which proscribe the vilification of one race by another and especially the vilification of minority groups in society. The Longford Report on pornography came to the conclusion that one of the main objections to it was its tendency to treat women as sub-human. And the objection to the pervasive combination of sex and violence today in literature, film and television is that it degrades all humanity to animal level and encourages people to treat each other as animals. To those who say that this is realistic our reply is that it is one-sided. Man is spirit and soul and body, and to portray him as body only is untrue and unreal. To those who say it is mere entertainment and does not matter, we reply in the words of Paul to the Corinthians that 'bad company ruins good morals'.[5] All those weak-minded people who are affected by films which debase human nature to animal level take away some of the freedom of those whom they subsequently treat with less respect. Three people collecting for the blind stood in the foyer of a Leicester Square cinema. The cinema was showing two films, a family film and a film of sex and violence. Almost everyone coming out of the family film gave the collectors a donation. Only one person coming out of the sex-and-violence film gave the collectors anything.

The law on blasphemy is an odd category of its own. If curses are meaningless, why do people use them? If people do not believe in God, why do they curse him with such eloquence? If curses make no difference to our fellows, then why do we curse them? The Christian who believes that we should love God and our fellows believes also that it is absolutely wrong to curse either,[6] and cannot see that the self-control necessary to bite back a curse does any harm to the person who has bitten it back or anything but good to the relationship with the person who might otherwise have been cursed.

Freedom of worship

This fourth freedom requires the discipline of tolerance. Christians in Northern Ireland have to remind themselves that those whose faith is different from their own may be mistaken but must still be treated as neighbours. When our Lord was asked 'Who is my neighbour?' he preached to the Jews the parable of the Good Samaritan.[7] There was a dispute between Jews and Samaritans as to whether the Samaritans were entitled to live in the land the Jews claimed as their own. They were regarded as a different race. They debated also whether the Samaritans' form of worship was correct and whether they should worship with the Jews at Jerusalem. But the kindly neighbour in Christ's story was a Samaritan; he was the one who looked after the Jew who had been beaten and robbed while the other Jews passed by on the other side of the road. That story is an object lesson in Christian tolerance.

Totalitarian states demand a medieval uniformity of belief within the state. Christianity, which started as a minority belief in the Roman Empire, never demanded that the Empire should have a uniform faith; but the Romans found it easier to govern citizens who were subject to common religious sanctions as well as common civil laws. As Christianity grew in strength, it was convenient to make it the common faith of the Empire. From the time of Constantine Christians allowed their faith to be made a convenience for rulers and allowed people without any faith whatever to be pressed into membership of the Christian church. As a result these outsiders took the church over and corrupted it. This mould was not broken until the Reformation and even then it took another hundred years for the Reformers to realize that church and state were separate and complementary.

Today the attempt to impose a uniform ideology comes from secular groups who are intolerant of other races or classes. In many countries Christians are back in the first century. Their most urgent need as a church is to secure freedom of worship from the ruling ideology.

The Christian concept of freedom

Those are the world's four freedoms. What is the Christian idea of freedom? The apostle Peter says of the world, 'They promise them freedom, but they themselves are slaves of corruption; for whatever overcomes a man, to that he is enslaved.'[8] And Paul talks of this slavery when he says, 'For I do not do the good I want, but the evil I do not want is what I do.'[9] But he tells the Christians, 'Where the Spirit of the Lord is, there is freedom.'[10] James talks of 'the perfect law, the law of liberty'.[11] This may sound paradoxical, but perhaps Christ himself explains it when he says 'No one can serve two masters; for either he will hate the one and love the other, or else he will be devoted to the one and despise the other. You cannot serve God and mammon.'[12]

Christ teaches that no-one is entirely free. If we do not have the spirit of Christ then we have the spirit of corruption. This will lead us inexorably downwards like the drugs which hook the junkie. At first he thinks he is free to take them or reject them, and by the time he finds he is not free, it is too late.

As the countries of Christendom slip away from their nominal allegiance to the Christian faith, we can see the spirit of corruption only too clearly at work. There is deterioration in human relationships. Unions are striking which have not struck for ten, twenty or even fifty years. There is a new bitterness in politics. There is a new mistrust which feeds the extremists and the separatists and at a time of greater equality in incomes and education there is more class consciousness than ever before. And in common rooms, board rooms and union executives people who have everything to gain by reasoned persuasion lose control of themselves and alienate those they need to influence. When they are asked why they allow themselves to make enemies in this way they will often tell you that they cannot help it. There is some power beyond their control which corrupts their relationships with their fellows. That is not freedom; that is bondage.

The consequence of everyone doing what is right in his own eyes is confusion and frustration. God the Creator has laid down laws for human relations and unless we observe these laws nothing can get done. We are trying to make an engine go without reading the instructions. To get anything done we need discipline. The elimination of poverty, disease and physical suffering, the provision of shelter, all require organized action and chains of command and trust between individuals. Business and government require a moral base, a general consensus, the rule of law, encouraging certainty and confidence. The constant plea of the business community to government is that they should provide an atmosphere of confidence. Without this trust the great wealth-producing machine of industrialized society grinds to a halt.

Christianity promises the freedom which comes from working with the divine order and not against it. Driving a car or riding a horse brings great freedom if we exercise the discipline required to master it. Only if we accept the discipline can we enjoy the freedom. Any great achievement requires discipline. The running of a great company or university requires enormous discipline and yet, because it is a creative job and always on the frontiers of human achievement, it brings enormous self-fulfilment. The same is true in science and in the arts.

The Christian faith is the route to this freedom because it gives a true understanding of man's relation to man and of man's relation to the Creator of the universe in which we live. Paul says, 'The wisdom of this world is folly with God.'[13] That is because it does not take into account this revealed knowledge. It insists that the only valid knowledge is what man can discover for himself and it will not accept what God has told us. But as the writer to the Hebrews says, quoting the prophet Jeremiah, God not only reveals this to the Christian but also promises, 'I will put my laws on their hearts, and write them on their minds.'[14] The Christian accepts God's revealed truth which he has tested and validated. This strengthening instinct for God's law begins to warn him of the corruption concealed behind the bland face of temptation.

But for the Christian, freedom is not an end in itself. For the man of the world freedom may be the right to satisfy his immediate instinct, but for the Christian freedom has a wider purpose. The Christian believes that man was made to glorify the God who created him in his own image. He does this by serving God and his fellows. And he serves by making the world a better place than he found it. Christian freedom, therefore, is bound up with the Christian doctrines of the divine calling, a belief that each one of us has been given talents to use and that we must use these talents to the full.

One of the talents God has given is the talent to teach the next generation, to guide them and set them on their way. There are few things in life more satisfying than this. The Bible story tells of the great pride which men and women took in their families, a pride and a joy which is strictly muted in this materialistic age.

Christians also want to serve their community. To begin with this will mean serving the church, which, as we have seen, is an immensely varied community of differing races and classes. Such service can be a source of great satisfaction. Paul, as he contemplated his own day-to-day experience of serving the churches, could comment, 'To me to live is Christ.'[15] But through the church the Christian will reach out also to the world around, and will seek to use his talents in the service of his fellows. Some will be called to relieve the wants and sufferings of their fellows; others will be involved in education; yet others in legislation and government. But whatever calling he has, the Christian knows that he is put there, not just to make money or to serve his own ambitions, but to fulfil a divine commission. He therefore brings to his work a dedication and determination for improvement which help to make society at every level a better place.

It is in this sense of fulfilment that the Christian finds, in the words of the Church of England collect, that God's service is 'perfect freedom'.

Notes

1. I chaired a NEDO investigation into value-added tax (which was published in 1969). One of the prime concerns of the investigation was the effect of 'self-policing' on tax morality. The fear was that the relatively high tax morality of the United Kingdom might be affected by including a major tax dependent largely on 'self-policing' and spot checks. The team visited four European countries operating VAT. In one of them the officials, when asked about the level of evasion, shrugged their shoulders expressively and said, 'If we knew that, we would collect the tax.' After discussion, their country was reported at an estimated evasion level of 20%. Companies taking over small businesses with a cash trade regularly find a large cash income not declared for tax. The law on taxation, like the law on picketing, or any other law, can be enforced only when there is general agreement that it is fair, and when there is strong public resentment when it is broken.

2. The Preacher in Ecclesiastes 10:16 mourns the country with weak government: 'Woe to you, O land, when your king is a child, and your princes feast in the morning!' The verdict of history seems to bear out the views of the Preacher. Countries seem to prosper under a strong and wise government, and to fall on evil times under a weak and indecisive one.

3. Matthew 12:36.

4. See the teaching about the tongue in James 3:5f.

5. 1 Corinthians 15:33.

6. Exodus 20:7, 'You shall not take the name of the Lord your God in vain.'

See also Deuteronomy 5:11. In Matthew 5:44 we are told to pray for those who persecute us. See also Luke 6:28 and Romans 12:14.

7. See Luke 10:29–37.   8. 2 Peter 2:19.   9. Romans 7:19.

10. 2 Corinthians 3:17.   11. James 1:25.

12. Matthew 6:24; Luke 16:13.

13. 1 Corinthians 3:19; *cf.* 1 Corinthians 1:18–25.

14. Hebrews 10:16; *cf.* Jeremiah 31:33.   15. Philippians 1:21.

For further reading

The Christian in Industrial Society

Sir Frederick Catherwood

The Christian attitude to work, wealth,
economics and politics; the social
responsibility of big business and the
trade unions; the authority and rights
of government; the Christian as an
employer; these are some of the issues
discussed in this book.

Large paperback, 144 pages

Is Revolution Change?

Edited by Brian Griffiths

Is violent revolution the answer to
society's problems? Is there a Christian
way? A symposium by an international
team of five authors, including
Sir Frederick Catherwood.

Pocketbook, 112 pages

Inter-Varsity Press, 38 De Montfort Street
Leicester LE1 7GP